HISTORY OF A ONE-ROOM SCHOOLHOUSE IN KNOX, NY

Covers: The background of the front cover is a page from the January 1844 Annual Report of the Trustees of School District Number 5 (formed partly out of the Town of Knox and partly out of the adjoining Town of New Scotland) to the Town Superintendant of Common Schools of each town. The background of the back cover is a page from the minutes of the October 1846 Annual Meeting of School District Number 5.

HISTORY OF A ONE-ROOM SCHOOLHOUSE IN KNOX, NY

School Board Minutes 1824-1905
Restoration of the Schoolhouse
Interviews with Former Students

Daniel A. Driscoll

Forward by Hon. John J. McEneny

Friends of Thacher State Park
c/o Emma Treadwell Thacher Nature Center
87 Nature Center Way
Voorheesville, NY 12186-2601
http://www.friendsofthacherpark.org

ISBN 978-1-312-67176-8

Published by:
Friends of Thacher State Park
c/o Emma Treadwell Thacher Nature Center
87 Nature Center Way
Voorheesville, NY 12186-2601
http://www.friendsofthacherpark.org

Distributed by:
Lulu Press, Inc.; 3101 Hillsborough St,
Raleigh, NC 27607
http://www.Lulu.com

CONTENTS

Forward

By Hon. John J. McEneny
Member of Assembly 1993 – 2012 &
Albany County Historian 1989 – 91

If we were to look for the iconic symbols which would best represent the early years of our fledgling American democracy, we would no doubt include the log cabin and the one room school house at the top of the list. For a farming people still taming the wilderness, the realities of rural isolation, poor transportation and harsh weather made centralized centers of education out of the question. The solution was to build simple one room structures to educate children within walking distance of their homes. Like the new national and state governments, they too were an experiment in self government. One room schools like Knox No. 5 were part of a uniquely diversified grass roots system of common school education, locally administered by trustees elected by their neighbors.

Primitive schoolhouses were first constructed of rough logs, like their builders' original farm homes. In time, both would be upgraded or replaced with frame or more substantial construction. The modest schoolhouses once dotted the landscape of our Helderberg Hill Towns; the town of Knox once had thirteen such structures. All are gone now, simply torn down, abandoned, or in some fortunate cases, converted to other uses like the subject of this book.

In Dan Driscoll's narrative of Knox Schoolhouse Number 5, three important stories are told. First, Dan offers a detailed account of how one community came together to save a late 19th century building from the ravages of time, and restored it so it could help tell its significant tale to future generations. Even more personally, the story includes the rich memories, both happy and otherwise, of some very senior former students, who had actually attended the schoolhouse before its closing in 1939. Their stories provide the warmth of human emotion through memories that are all too often the most perishable elements of our history. Finally, the transcript of the actual handwritten ledger book of the school district from 1824 through 1905, saved by the descendant of an early trustee, and now held by the Town of New Scotland Historical Society, presents us with a very special archival survivor rarely seen by most researchers.

The journal transcripted here was begun nearly two centuries ago, when almost all of America was rural and self government by common citizens was a bold and still unproven experiment. Ironically, elected trustees who committed themselves to empowering the next generation and the future with a basic educational foundation, often lacked the same sound education they wished to impart to their children. The quality of the script and spelling may vary, but the careful narration of trustee election results, assessment of taxes, hiring of teachers, the preoccupation with firewood to be supplied to the single pot bellied stove, and acknowledgements that half the student body might be absent on any given day, gives us a remarkably detailed look on a system of education that made our country.

This book reminds us that the one room school house somehow managed to contribute beyond its modest means to creating a population with good basic skills, a strong work ethic and pride in their American citizenship. We are all the better for it.

1
Introduction

The Town of Knox is in the northwest corner of Albany County, New York; it is a rural "township" in the Helderberg Mountains about ten miles west of the city of Albany. Knox School District Number 5 was in the southeast corner of the town on the edge of the Helderberg Escarpment. The last schoolhouse used by the District is still standing at its original location on Ketcham Road.

The book, Records of School District No. 5 in the Town of Knox, was loaned to the New Scotland Historical Association by Marty Milner of Ketcham Road, Knox, NY. His elderly friend and neighbor Dave Sagendorf gave Mr. Milner the book. Mr. Sagendorf was a student at Knox School #5 around 1930 and obtained the book from his grandfather, Frank Pitcher, the last School Board member to use the book (Franklin Pitcher was Clerk in 1905, the last meeting recorded). Mr. Sagendorf was interviewed as part of the schoolhouse project; that interview, along with interviews with other former students and users of the schoolhouse, are summarized in Appendix I.

The book measures about 6 ½ by 8 inches and is about 5/8 inch thick. The covers are 1/16 inch thick cardboard. The binding is sewn, with leather spine covering. There are 74 leaves (148 pages). All of the writing is in pen and ink unless otherwise noted. Some of the leaves are loose, and, based on remnants of leaves remaining in the binding, there appear to have been several leaves torn out of the book. Initially the transcript of the book was

made keeping the order of pages as received by the New Scotland Historical Association. The text was then re-arranged in chronological order. Only a few of the loose leaves were found to be out of order. However, many of the entries were not in chronological order; many later entries were written on blank pages throughout the book (and there are still a few blank pages throughout the book). The transcript is Appendix II.

The minutes of the annual meetings are complete except for the years 1833, 1838, and 1898. Most of the early meetings are in relatively good chronological order. Since the 1832 and 1834 annual meetings are on the front and back of a single leaf, and since the 1837 annual meeting and the first meeting in 1839 are on the front and back of a single leaf, it appears most likely that the minutes for the 1833 and 1838 annual meetings were not recorded (assuming the meetings were held). Sometime after the 1897 annual meeting, there was a special meeting at which it was decided to build a new (the still standing) schoolhouse; that meeting was adjourned "until the first tuesday in August 1898." The next meeting recorded was August 1899; perhaps construction of the new schoolhouse interfered with the August 1898 annual meeting.

This transcription uses Historic Cherry Hill's "Guide for Recording Quotations" by Maxine Lorang, which is based on the Chicago Manual of Style, 13th edition. Editorial comments (corrections, clarifications, and explanations) are in brackets. Irregular spelling, grammar, punctuation, and capitalizations are carefully preserved; there are so many such irregularities that only a few of the more potentially troublesome are followed by "[sic]" to indicate that they are not transcription errors. Page layout and lists are also preserved to the extent possible. Missing or illegible words, letters or numbers that can be provided with reasonable confidence are followed by a question mark and placed in brackets, otherwise, a blank space about the size of the omitted material is enclosed in brackets.

2
Other Sources of Information

Before examining the contents of the records of the school board meetings, it will be useful to examine the historical context of those meetings. Therefore, other sources of related information as well as relevant historical events will be examined in the following paragraphs.

The Knox, New York Sesquicentennial booklet (privately published in 1972; Frieda Saddlemire, Chair of the Publication Committee, and republished in 2014 by the Knox Historical Society) gives the following information about schools; references cited include Amasa Parker's Landmarks of Albany County and Howell and Tenney's History of the County of Albany. In 1789, the year after the federal Constitution was ratified, the New York State Legislature authorized that in each town two lots of the public state land be set apart for gospel and school purposes. The Common School Act of 1812 authorized the establishment of common, or public schools.

The earliest schools were crude structures of unpeeled logs and dirt floors, topped with lean-to roofs covered with bark. Eventually, as other work permitted, the floors were covered with white pine and the bark roofs were replaced with shakes. The children in those schools ranged from six to sixteen years; they recited their lessons aloud; consequently the schools became known as "blab schools." As the Town grew, so did the schools, and the log "blab schools" gave way to small frame buildings.

Knox became a town in February 1822; it had been part of the Town of Berne which became a town in 1795. By 1886, Knox had thirteen school districts; each elected its own trustees, clerk, and tax collector. The trustees were charged with hiring the teacher, supervising the school, and providing for the supply and maintenance of the building and its equipment. By that time, the schools were supported by a local tax that varied according to the value of an individual's taxable property. The teachers were then paid thirty dollars per month; they were required not only to teach a wide variety of subjects to pupils of various ages and abilities within a single room, but also to clean the room, and to build and maintain fires in the wood-burning stove.

The Beers map of 1866 shows that Knox School House No. 5 was located on a road (now called Ketcham Road) just north of Thompsons Lake. The figure below shows the southeast corner of the Beers map, the area around School House No. 5. According to Gary L. Donhardt (Indian Ladder – A History of Life in the Helderbergs, Donhardt and Daughters Publishers, Collierville, TN, 2001, p.150) the school was sometimes called the Secor School.

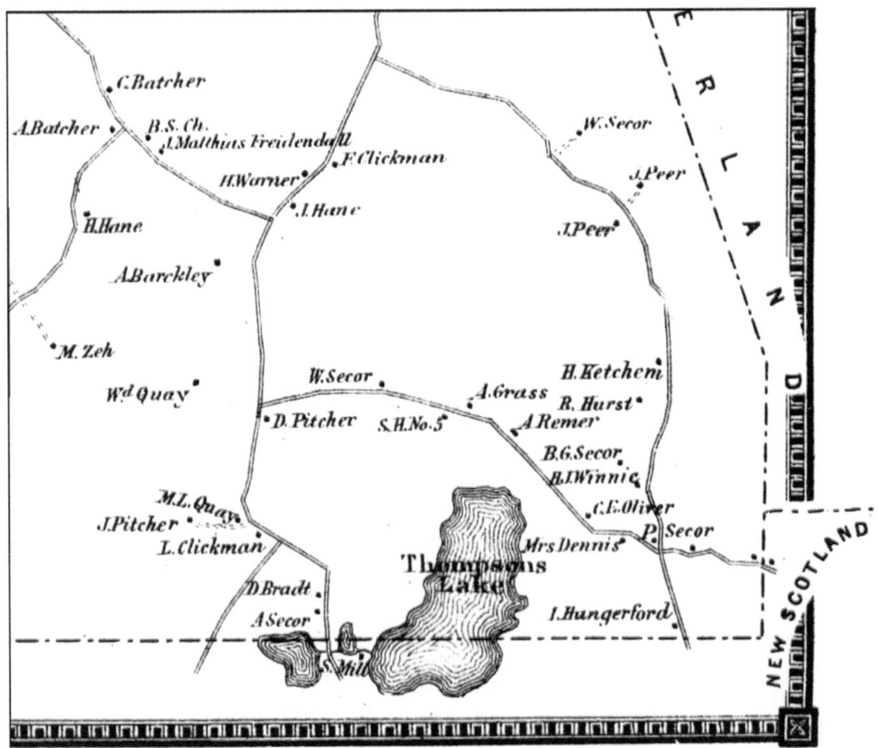

The Sesquicentennial booklet explains that District No. 5, with its schoolhouse at Ketcham Road and Boys Club Lane (later called Stan Levine Drive, now Nature Center Way) became part of the Berne-Knox Central School system in 1951. For the ten years before that happened, 1940 to 1950, the children of the district were driven to the Altamont School by Alta Salisbury. The Berne-Knox School system was established in 1932 as a junior high school; in 1933 it was expanded to include elementary and high school as well.

The Sesquicentennial booklet states that in 1886 "District No. 5 had 31 school age children of whom 27 were enrolled." But the average daily attendance was only 8.5. The school was valued at $500, and its 25 volume library was valued at $25. Teachers included Margaret Clickman (1912), Miss McCormick (1912), Mrs. Earl Warner (1916-18), Millard Whipple, and Fanny Ellis (1926-27).

The Directory of Albany and Schenectady Counties for 1870-71 list the following farmers (who are mentioned in the School Board Records) and the acreage they had:

Ketcham, Henry	100 acres
Ketchman (sic), Newton	63
Ketchman (sic), Wm & Alonzo	100
Pier, Jacob	85
Hungerford, John	132

Isaac Hungerford was listed as a retired farmer, age 74.

The book Landmarks of Albany County New York (Edited by Amasa J. Parker of Albany, NY; Published by D.Mason & Co., Syracuse, NY, 1897) has the following information about the Town of Knox. Page 537 - The records of the Town were burned in 1850. Page 541 – In the late 1700's there are thought to have been two primitive log school houses, one in Knoxville (Knox hamlet) and the other in West Township; there were 12 districts in 1860, thirteen in 1880, and 12 again in 1897 with a schoolhouse in each. "Knox, Guilderland, Colonie, and Green Island form the third school commissioner district of the county." Page 542 – Concerning the building of the Thompson's Lake Reformed Church the book says: "In 1839 dissentions again arose and the Reformed members withdrew and built the church at Secor's."

3
Relevant Historical Events

As the records of the school board meetings are read, it is helpful to be aware of concurrent historical events that may have had an impact on the Knox community. An unlikely source for that history is the book Stone by Stone – The Magnificent History of New England's Stone Walls by Robert M. Thorson, Walker & Company, New York, 2002. The story of stone walls is intertwined with the story of farming. The period from about the beginning of the American Revolution in 1775 to about 1825 was a relatively prosperous time for farming and a period of intense stone wall building.

However, early in the 19th century things began to change for farming. Thorson refers to the decade from the Market Panic of 1819 to 1829 as a "watershed decade" for the family farm (and for stone walls). It began a transition from a largely agricultural society to an industrial nation. The orator Daniel Webster set the tone in 1825 when he said "Our proper business is improvement. Let our age be the age of improvement." In 1825 the Erie Canal was completed, opening the way for competition from farms in the Great Lakes region. Construction of the first overland railroad in 1829 enticed many farmers to move to richer farmlands in the West. Another Panic in 1837 was accompanied by a crash in agricultural prices. The Homestead Act of 1862 gave away rich farmland enticing more farmers to move west.

Abraham Lincoln was president from 1861 to 1865. During the Civil War from 1861 to 1865 many young men left farming never to return. After the war, rather than return to the economic and physical hardship of the farm, many took jobs in factories.

The Anti-Rent Rebellion was a more immediate concern for the residents of Knox. According to Henry Christman's book Tin Horns and Calico (Hope Farm Press, Cornwallville, NY 1975), it started at a meeting in neighboring Berne in July 1839 "when the people of the hilltowns determined to throw off the yoke of bondage to lifelong servitude under the patroon system." A new "Declaration of Independence" was sent to the patroon, Stephen Van Rensselaer IV; in response he had the sheriff draw up writs of ejectment against the leaders. In late August 1839, an undersheriff delivered the first writ to Isaac Hungerford. (Isaac Hungerford was elected a trustee of Knox School #5 in 1828 and served in various capacities through 1851.)

Christman reports that Hungerford responded "You'd better get home and be in some other business --- I warn you as a friend to go no further. You can't go through this country with patroon papers and get home a live man." Hungerford then drew a long knife from his belt and said, "I'm warning you! There are hundreds like me. We'd as soon die as not, if we have to."

In 1844, Daniel Webster, when asked his opinion on the legality of the patroon system, said, "If I had time I would tear that manor into shoestrings."

In May 1844, anti-rent leaders from three counties met at the home of John Gallup in East Berne. They decided to meet force with force, agreeing to form a band of protectors with Calico Indian costumes as a disguise, reminiscent of the Boston Tea Party. Soon, a well-trained group of about 10,000 was formed as the movement spread to other leasehold counties. Despite bloody conflict and legal setbacks over the next year or two, the Calico Indian resistance was one factor that led to the demise of the patroon system. One of the last battles of the Rebellion took place in 1866 at Peter Warner's farm on Warner's Lake Road in Knox, shown in the photo above; the farm is less than two miles from Knox School #5. According to Christman, the Anti-Rent Rebellion also "led directly to the passage of the federal Homestead Act of 1862 which opened the West to the people."

The farms that remained prosperous during the decline of the family farm were the ones near industrial centers or areas of tourism. Thompson's Lake was a popular tourist destination according to Gary L. Donhardt (Indian Ladder – A History of Life in the Helderbergs, Donhardt and Daughters Publishers, Collierville, TN, 2001). Two hotels were built at the south end of the lake, about a mile from Knox School No.5: Lake View House around 1876, and the Grove Hotel in 1884. Donhardt reports that Harry Warner supplied 40 to 50 quarts of milk a day to Lake View House, "and played the Jew's harp in the evenings for the pleasure of the hotel guests." The popularity of the area continued into the early 1900's, but gradually the tourist trade dropped off, due in part to the automobile that made other tourist destinations accessible.

The book Indian Ladder has a photo of John McWilliams' house (which was close to the Park Office at Thacher Park). McWilliams was a trustee of Knox School No.5 beginning in 1835; he was from the Town of New Scotland. It also has a photo of Jemima Ketcham; she and her husband Ambrose Ketcham "converted their home into a boarding house capable of holding at least 12 over-night guests and 25 patrons for Sunday dinner." The book also has a photo of their home which they called High Peak House. Ambrose Ketcham was the librarian of Knox School No.5 beginning in 1873.

Donhardt gives a short biography of Simon P. Winne (page 68); he includes a picture of Simon and his wife Margaret. Simon Winne was a trustee of Knox School No.5 beginning in 1891. Simon Winne was also a deacon of the Second Dutch Reformed Church of Berne (Thompson's Lake Reformed Church). Donhardt has an interesting story about what happened after it was charged that Deacon Winne had "profaned the name of God."

An article on Migration in the 1970 Encyclopedia Britannica singles out the 19th century as the most important modern era of migration, with an overwhelming majority immigrating to the United States; large scale movement to America continued until the US Immigration act of 1924. The largest number of people came from the British Isles, followed by Germany and other European countries. Migration tended to occur in "waves" about 18 to 20 years apart. The four clear peaks in migration were – 1844-54, 1863-73, 1881-88, and 1903-13. Each of the four peak periods was primarily a rural exodus, much of it stimulated by progress in US agriculture and the advance in ocean and rail transport. The Great Potato Famine occurred during the first peak and resulted in an influx of Irish farmers. During the period from 1849 to 1854 at least 80% of the immigrants were from Ireland and Germany. The movement out of Germany was due more to economic pressure in the countryside than to the political troubles of 1848 (when there were revolutions in several European countries).

4
History of the County of Albany

The book History of the County of Albany From 1609 To 1886 by George R. Howell and Jonathan Tenney (New York, 1886) has a wealth of information about the County of Albany in general and the Town of Knox in particular. Jonathan Tenney was a Deputy State Superintendent of Public Instruction and a resident of Albany County.

On pages 268 and 269 of the book Tenney comments: "The educational growth of our County has been very rapid during the last one hundred years, and especially so during the last fifty years." "It must be admitted that these influences have slowly entered into our country towns. We have no doubt that the manorial system, so long existing in these towns, has been the chief paralyzing cause. It made men groveling and ambitionless. A better day for these beautiful valleys and hills, these homes and villages, is lifting. Schools and schoolhouses are better, and men and women of intelligence and influence are multiplying."

On page 77, talking about the Town of Knox, Tenney says, "The anti-rent feeling in this town was general and intense. Most of the farmers held manorial leases, and resisted the collection of rents with inflexible determination. --- No towns, perhaps, showed more active resistance than Berne and Knox."

On pages 264 and 265 the following information is given about education. On April 7, 1795, the State Legislature appropriated the sum of 20,000 pounds annually for the term of five years, for encouraging and maintaining schools in the state. Of this sum, 1,590 pounds, or $3,975, was allotted to Albany County. For the year 1820, the county had 155 common schools; Berne had 30. On May 26, 1841 the legislature required County Boards of Supervisors to appoint biennially a County Superintendent of Common Schools; on November 13, 1847 the office was abolished leaving school supervision to Town Superintendents. As was mentioned in Landmarks of Albany County, Knox was in the 3rd School

Commissioner District for the County; commissioners from Knox included John H. Sand (1856), George H. Quay (1864 and 1870), and Charles E. Sturges (1882).

Howell and Tenney give the following population data for the towns of Berne and Knox; recall that Knox did not become a town until February 1822.

Date	US Census Knox	US Census Berne
1810		5134
1820		5531
1830	2189	3607
1840	2143	3740
1850	2021	3441
1860	2025	3065
1870	1656	2562
1880	1694	2616

Date	NYS Census Knox	NYS Census Berne
1814		4447
1835	2262	3956
1845	2161	3667
1855	1888	3206
1865	1809	2851
1875	1641	2565

It is clear that the population of the towns decreased from 1835 to 1875; there is a hint that the population may have begun to increase in 1880. According to the US Census Bureau, the population of Knox was 2647 in 2000 and 2692 in 2010. The population of Berne was 2846 in 2000 and 2794 in 2010. A factor that may have influenced population in the 1800s (and perhaps the difficulty of obtaining firewood) – Howell and Tenney mention (page 869) that in 1886, the Town of Knox was "almost stripped of its timber."

5
Contents of the Minutes

The book, Records of School District No. 5 in the Town of Knox, covers the period from 1824 to 1905. It contains several different types of records including – minutes of annual meetings (except for 1833, 38, and 98); minutes of various special meetings; annual reports to the Commissioner of Common Schools (for 1830, 32, 39, 40 and 44); library records for 1840; various receipts for money paid or received; lists of families required to supply firewood; and other miscellaneous lists, calculations, and notes.

Knox became a town in February 1822, separating from the Town of Berne. Knox School District No. 5 is in the southeast corner of the town, adjacent to both Berne and New Scotland. The first school board meeting recorded in the Records of School District No.5 (October 1824) was about two and a half years after Knox became a town.

Initially the meeting participants were described as "freeholders and inhabitants." A freeholder was a person who actually owned their land; it could be sold or passed on to descendents. People living under the patroon system, however, could not own their land; they paid annual rent and were required to provide a certain amount of labor for the patroon each year. The last use of the phrase "freeholders and inhabitants" was at a meeting on November 1, 1845; on November 15, 1845 and thereafter, the meeting participants were described as "legal voters." The previous year had been one of the most violent of the Anti-Rent Rebellion, with armed resistance by bands of Calico Indians, so the distinction between freeholders and inhabitants was probably a sore issue.

Another important change took place in January 1839. In 1835, John McWilliams, a resident of New Scotland was elected a trustee of the District. He was elected trustee again in 1837, and remained in that office until 1853. Before the January 1839 annual report, the District was referred to as "School District No.5 in the Town of Knox." Beginning in January 1839 the District was "School District

No.5 formed partly out of the said town, and partly out of the adjoining town of New Scotland." The January 1839 annual report is also the first mention of financial support for the District from the Town of New Scotland. And in subsequent years, John McWilliams is occasionally listed as the trustee who "received public money" from the New Scotland Commissioner of Common Schools. In 1839, for example, the amount received from the Commissioners of Common Schools was $45.37 from Knox and $3.38 from New Scotland.

There is some financial information in the Records of School District No.5. During the early years, the amount of money received from the Commissioners of Common Schools is listed. For about half of the years between 1824 and 1849, payments to teachers are recorded. There is also some spotty information about the cost of a cord of wood, the cost of fencing, and other items.

One of the more consistent things discussed at the trustee meetings was the supply of wood to heat the schoolhouse; the school used five to six and a half cords per year for the years 1851, 65, 69, and 77. They tried different methods to assure a supply of wood. Sometimes each family was required to supply a share of the wood; occasionally a list in the minutes gives the names of the families in the district and the amount of wood they were required to supply (1/4, 1/3 or 1/2 cord). Other times the trustees decided that the fuel would be "raised by tax," and one individual was paid to supply the wood. In 1845, the first year the wood was furnished by tax, the total cost of firewood for the year was $9; in 1904 the cost was $15. The trustees gradually became more careful to specify the quality of the wood, specifying that it be "fitted for the stove" and in 1892 requiring that it be "dry hard maple wood."

There is occasional mention of a tax on the residents, usually to pay for schoolhouse construction or schoolhouse maintenance as shown in the table below (the taxes listed are special one-time taxes and do not include any annual tax for firewood). In 1875, there was mention of equalizing the valuation of property for one of the residents, and in September 1890 the tax was actually specified as $0.50/$100 valuation. Beginning in 1893, there was a gradually increasing tax levied for school purposes or teachers' wages (apparently to supplement the "public money" from the Commissioners of Common Schools, since the trustees seemed to have had difficulty hiring teachers in the later years).

Annual Meeting	**Tax**	**Purpose of Tax**
1824 October	$ 5.00	Repair
1825 December	$ 5.00	"
1829 November	$ 6.00	"
1832 October	$ 50.00	Moving & rebuilding
1836 November	$ 50.00	Rebuilding
1839 October	$ 10.00	Repair
1840 October	$ 10.00	"
1845 November	$12.87 1/2	"
1851 January	$ 30.00	Support of school
1851 October	$ 25.00	Teachers wages
1852 October	$ 210.00	Building the school
1890 September	$.50/100val.	Repair
1893 August	$ 50.00	School purposes
1894 August	$ 75.00	" and painting
1895 August	$ 50.00	Teachers wages
1896 August	$ 50.00	"
1897 August	$ 60.00	"
1899 August	$ 120.00	School purposes
1901 August	$ 125.00	"
1902 August	$ 100.00	"
1903 August	$ 125.00	"
1904 August	$ 125.00	"
1905 August	$ 125.00	"

The most consistent topic of discussion at trustee meetings was the election of the trustees, District Clerk, Tax Collector, and, beginning in 1839, the librarian. There was a total of 75 people who served in elected positions during the years recorded in the Records of

School District No.5. From 1824 to 1843, three trustees were elected for one-year terms. Beginning in 1844, the three trustees were elected for staggered three-year terms. There was occasionally some ambiguity in the minutes about who was trustee. Apparently the trustees themselves were occasionally unsure; in 1858 and again in 1883, after periods of ambiguity, they re-initiated the staggered three-year terms. In 1859, there were only two trustees. In 1899, no results were given for the election of trustees, but the clerk, collector and librarian results were given. From 1900 to 1905, it is not clear whether there was more than a single trustee, and the office of librarian was no longer mentioned.

In February 1839, a special meeting was held to elect the first librarian. At the same meeting, rules were set for the operation of the library, including fines for overdue books. By the end of that year, the library had 46 books. In 1840, the same individual was both clerk and librarian, so the records of the library were kept in the same book as the meeting minutes; for that year the library records include the title and number of the book, the borrower, the date it was borrowed, the date it was returned, and the condition of the book. The library had a separate allocation from the Commissioners of Common Schools. However, occasionally that money was diverted to other purposes, for example, to supplement the teacher's salary; the first time that was done, in 1841, the trustees questioned whether it was allowed by law.

Twice, the Records of School District No.5 listed the text books used in the school – in 1844 and again in 1877.

The annual reports, filed in conformity with the Statute for the Support of Common Schools, are recorded in the minutes for the years 1830, 32, 39, 40, and 44. The reports give information such as the length of time the school was in session, the number of students taught, whether the teacher had obtained a certificate of qualification, the amount of money received from the Commissioners of Common Schools, whether the school had been inspected by the Superintendent, and the number of school-age children listed by family. A page from the annual report for January 1844 is shown below; (it also serves as the background for the cover of this book).

Of Trustees of School District where the Distri
is formed out of two or more azoining towns
to the Town Superintendant of Common School
of each town from which said District is
in part composed — — —
To the Town Superintendant of Common School
of the Town of Knox — —
We the trustees of school district number
five formed partly out of said town and
partly out of the azoining town of New
Scotland do in conformity with the statute
relating to Common School certify and report
That the school house in said district is
situated in the town of Knox — —
That the whole time any school has been
kept in our district during the year ending
on the date hereof and since the date of the
last report for said district is Ten months
and that the time during said year and since
the date of said last last report such
school has been kept by Teachers after
obtaining a certificate of qulification
according to law is Ten monthe

The lists of school-age children by family in the annual reports give an indication of the number of families in the school district and their names. A similar indication is also given by a list of taxes due for 1837, and by firewood lists for 1851, 65, 69, and 77. Less reliable are several lists of voters at the annual meetings. Consistent with the State and federal census data, the number of families in the district decreased steadily between 1830 when there were 26 families listed and 1865 when only 11 families were listed; and it shows that the population may have begun to increase in 1869 and 1877. Only one family, Isaac Hungerford, appears in both the 1830 and 1865 lists, and only four other family names are common to the two lists (Pier, Reamer, Secor, and Winney). The new family names in 1865 are Bradt, Cornelius, Ketcham, and Oliver. The economic hardships for farmers, the enticements for farmers to move west (including the Homestead Act of 1862), and the Civil and Anti-Rent wars apparently had taken their toll.

6
Students and Teachers

Several former students from Knox School No. 5 still lived in the area and were interviewed as part of the effort to restore the school; a summary of the interviews will be found in Appendix I. The former students are: Pauline (Salisbury) Williman; her brother Bill Salisbury; Isabelle (Quay) Baker; Susie (Secor) Livingston; and Dave Sagendorf. Pauline, Bill, and Isabelle still lived on Ketcham Road when the interviews were conducted. Pauline is a member of the Helderberg Kiwanis Club and visited the school occasionally during its restoration. Dave lived on Ketcham Road but was in the Daughters of Sarah Nursing Home in Albany at the time of the interview; his sister Christina lived out of state. Susie lived in New Salem. According to the former students, the school property included the schoolhouse itself, a woodshed, and two small outhouses.

The Records of School District No.5 gives the names of several of the teachers who taught at the school. Additional names are given in the Knox, New York Sesquicentennial booklet, and still more names were obtained during the interviews with former students. Although not complete by any means, the following is a list, in chronological order, compiled from all of those sources.

Helem Mead	1824 – 25
Alpheus Persons	1827
Datus E. Tyler	1828
Hezekiah Reynolds	1828 – 29, 1831
Henry Ogsberry	1830
Jemima VanSchaack	1840
C. Farley	1841
Harriet Phillips	1843
William Ketcham	1876 –
Adelia Secor	1904
Margaret Clickman	1912
Miss McCormick	1912

Mrs. Earl Warner	1916 – 18
Millard Whipple	
Fanny Ellis	1926 – 27
Miss Blake	1928 – 30
Ella (Schultes) Scrafford	1930 –
Edith Ketcham	1932
Venita Davis	1935
Miss Mabel Rivenburg	1936
Mrs. Filkins	1939

Pauline Williman said that Ellis, Blake, Davis, and Rivenburg all boarded with the Salisburys while they taught. Miss Blake had a disability that made it difficult for her to walk. Venita Davis taught for only a few months; she then married Harvey Way, Jr., Pauline's cousin. Miss Rivenburg was an older woman from Quaker Street. Ella Schultes was the daughter of Howard Schultes; she married Ralph Scrafford, the Berne Highway Superintendent. The photo shows Fanny Ellis at her desk in the Knox School #5 classroom. Additional information about Fanny Ellis will be found in the interview with Pauline Williman

The school year was divided into the winter and summer schools; in 1850 the winter and summer schools were each specified as being three-months long. Sometimes teachers were paid equal amounts for the terms (in 1830 for example); during other years the teacher was paid twice the amount for winter school as for summer school (in 1839 for example). In the early years, the salary was about $5 per month; in 1849 it was raised to $10 per month. By 1886, according to the Knox, New York Sesquicentennial Booklet, the pay was $30 per month.

7
Location of the School Buildings

When Knox became a town in February 1822, there must have been a period of transition as the former residents of Berne created or reorganized needed municipal functions. Knox School District No. 5, in the far southeast corner of the town near both Berne and New Scotland, apparently continued to use the same schoolhouse the District residents had used when they were part of Berne. At the very first recorded school board meeting in October 1824, the trustees passed a resolution to raise five dollars by tax to repair the schoolhouse.

And that schoolhouse seems to have been in the Town of Berne. The Beers map of 1866 shows that Isaac Hungerford, whose family was in the new Knox School District No.5, lived just north of the Berne-Knox town line on what is now Suto Road (apparently called the newroad in 1832). At the 1832 meeting of the school board, the trustees resolved to raise fifty dollars by tax to take down, move, and rebuild the schoolhouse. One of the trustees at that meeting was Simon Secor. The schoolhouse was to be moved only 500 yards north to a site on the public highway called "the newroad on the line between Simon Secor and Isaac Hungerford," presumably moving the schoolhouse into the Town of Knox.

That move, apparently, was never made. In 1834 the trustees resolved to move the schoolhouse to a site near the house of Isaac Ostrander. And in July 1836 they resolved to move the schoolhouse to a site on the land of Jacob A. Hellenbeck. There was some unspecified work done on the schoolhouse later that year, but several meetings in early 1837 were devoted to the details of raising (by tax) the money to move the schoolhouse. But even then the schoolhouse may not have been moved – in 1839 and 1840 additional taxes were levied (ten dollars each year) to repair the schoolhouse. In 1845 it was resolved to raise another ten dollars for schoolhouse repairs.

Finally, in 1852, the Superintendents of Common Schools of the two towns gave their opinion that "the removal of the site of the schoolhouse in said district is necessary." At the April 1852 school board meeting, the trustees voted for a new site "on the bush lot of William Secor on the road leading from Adam Reamers to William Secors on the south side of said road" and 125 yards west of a barn owned by Andrew Grass. Furthermore, at that meeting, the trustees were authorized to build the schoolhouse, and later that year, the trustees voted two hundred dollars for that purpose. As the Beers map of 1866 shows, the schoolhouse was actually built on that site.

At a special meeting in April 1853, the trustees met at the schoolhouse and decided to build a fence "on Saturday the 30th day of April 1853." So apparently the new schoolhouse was complete by that time. It was not very long before repairs were needed – only seventeen years later they needed a new roof on the schoolhouse, and in 1882 they decided to build a (replacement?) fence around three sides of the schoolhouse. Additional repairs were done in 1885 and 1890.

In August 1892, the trustees decided to sell the schoolhouse rather than repair it anymore, and to build a new schoolhouse. However, in September of that year, they voted to paint the outside of the schoolhouse with two coats of paint. They also resolved that "the ceiling be shellacked inside and then covered and finished with hard oil, the casings to be painted and varnished, and doors [be] stained and varnished."

At an undated meeting (probably in 1898), the trustees sold the old schoolhouse to William Secor for thirty dollars. They resolved to build a new schoolhouse "on the old site with the exception of additional grounds which Wm. J. Secor has agreed to give." The old site (starting in 1852 or 1853) was on William Secor's bush lot; the gift presumably increased the size of the schoolhouse property. The new schoolhouse was built sometime between the August 1897 and August 1899 annual meetings. As mentioned in the Introduction, there are no minutes for the August 1898 annual meeting (if one was held); construction of the schoolhouse may have interfered.

Isabelle (Quay) Baker, who went to the school beginning in about 1920, recalls that the woodshed was replaced by a larger one while she was there. So the current woodshed was probably built in the 1920s.

Schoolhouse No. 5 was kept in its original state until 1971, when it was converted into a dwelling. From about 1975 to about 1987, the building was used as a meeting place for the Helleberg Coon Club; Earl Wagoner, former president of the Club, was also interviewed (see Appendix I).

The New York State Department of Parks, Recreation and Historic Preservation purchased the property in October of 1999; at that time, the school building and woodshed were on the property, but the two outhouses had been removed. In 2001, the Kiwanis Club of the Helderbergs offered to partner with Parks to restore the school and woodshed; with the help of the community, Kiwanis began the restoration in June 2003.

8
Restoration of the Schoolhouse

New York State Department of Parks, Recreation and Historic Preservation (Parks) is the current owner of the school. After it acquired the school in 1999, Parks put plywood over the doors and windows of the schoolhouse and woodshed to minimize vandalism. In July 2001, at the opening of the Emma Thacher Nature Center, a member of the Friends of Thacher Park, Fred Schroeder, called the author's attention to the schoolhouse; we agreed that it would be a valuable community project to restore this historically important building.

Fred Schroeder, before retiring, was the director of the Albany Boys Club and the director of Camp Thacher on Thompsons Lake. He was an enthusiastic member of the Friends of Thacher Park. Fred and his wife Martha provided the funds for NY State to build and endow the Emma Treadwell Thacher Nature Center at Thompsons Lake State Park on the grounds of the former Albany Boys Club Camp Thacher.

The author, a member of the Helderberg Kiwanis Club, proposed that the Club take the lead to restore the school; they agreed. After obtaining permission and guidance from Parks, the Kiwanis Club, with the assistance of the Berne-Knox community and in partnership with Parks, began physical restoration of the schoolhouse and woodshed on June 22, 2003. Selkirk Cogen Partners, LP provided a grant of $750 to buy materials needed for the restoration (cedar roofing, furring strips, etc.)

On that first workday, a crew of 13 worked for four hours clearing weeds and removing the woodshed roof. Each summer, from 2003 thru 2008, we had 8 or 9 workdays involving 16 to 20 different people (both Kiwanians and other members of the community) working to restore the school, a total of about 200 man-hours each summer.

Since the schoolhouse roof was metal and in good condition, the schoolhouse itself was in stable condition. Initial attention was therefore directed to the woodshed. The woodshed roof was the original cedar shake roof and was rotten with gaping holes. The rest of the woodshed was in stable condition except for a few rotted boards. The tasks for the summer of 2003 were therefore to replace the woodshed roof and individual rotted boards. That work was completed by October 2003.

Also in the summer of 2003, Marty Milner informed Kiwanis that the original school desks were in an outbuilding at the Edwards farm (also owned by Parks). So the desks were retrieved and restoration was begun on the desks.

During the site work, we were careful to preserve any artifacts found; the only things found were a small doll's head and a button, which were given to Parks. During summer 2005, Parks itself did an archaeological study of the property and found a few more minor artifacts. Historic photographs of the interior of the schoolroom show that a potbelly stove originally stood in the middle of the schoolroom.

That stove could not be found, but Kiwanis obtained a nearly identical stove that was placed in the schoolroom after it was restored.

In September 2004, Parks applied to have the school (and woodshed) put on the National Register of Historic Places. The application was successful, and in June 2005 Parks notified the Town of Knox that the "referenced property has been listed on the National Register of Historic Places." The notification explains that the "listing" recognizes the importance of the property to the history of our country and provides the property with a measure of protection.

The Albany Times Union published an article about the school on October 6, 2005 with a follow-up article on April 23, 2006 mentioning that it is the only building in the Town of Knox to be placed on the National Register.

Schoolhouse - The schoolhouse seemed to be in stable condition when Kiwanis began restoration work. A fair amount of work had been done on the schoolhouse, probably in the 1970's or 80's when it was used as a residence for a while, and then as a meeting place for a hunting club, the Helleberg Coon Club. The original cedar shake roof had been covered or replaced by a metal roof that appeared to be in good condition; some of the rotten cedar shakes can still be seen in the attic under the metal roof.

At about the same time (1980's), the sill plate along the north side (street side) of the building had been replaced with what appears to be a 24-foot long railroad tie. In the process of replacing the sill plate, the building apparently slipped off its foundation and slid about a foot to the south, and concrete was poured on the south side to replace the foundation. Some flooring had been replaced by plywood, rotting floor joists were reinforced and a layer of oak tongue-and-groove flooring had been installed in the south side of the schoolroom.

During the summer of 2004, we removed the old flooring (three layers) from the schoolhouse. Most of the original flooring (wide tongue-tongue/groove-groove pine planks), the middle layer of flooring (narrow tongue & groove Douglas fir), the floor joists and sill plates were rotted. During 2005, the floor joists were removed, the building was jacked-up, the rubble foundation was rebuilt on the south, east and west sides, and the rotted sill plates were replaced with hemlock (custom-cut by Stempel Sawmill). In the process, the original siding was saved for reuse. Also, several intact pieces of hand-hewn floor joists, several pieces of the original wide pine flooring, and several pieces of the Douglas fir flooring (showing marks where the student desks were screwed down) were saved for display.

The brick chimney on the west side of the building was perfectly straight and passed through a cut-out in the eaves. It was therefore clear that the chimney had been built after the building slipped off its foundation (in the 1980's). After evaluating the chimney, Parks removed the chimney in 2005 and repaired the cut-out in the eaves in 2006. Also in 2006, Kiwanis, with the help of community members, installed a vapor barrier covered with crushed stone, replaced the floor joists (custom-cut by Stempel Sawmill), installed tongue & groove plywood underlayment, and replaced damaged siding.

By 2006, the $750 grant received from Selkirk Cogen Partners was depleted. We reapplied to Selkirk and were given a second grant of $500. In addition, we applied to Home Depot and were given $100 in gift cards (which helped pay for the underlayment), and the Kiwanis Club sponsored a community supper at Camp Pinnacle, raising $255 for the schoolhouse project.

The work we did on the school in 2007 was guided by Parks Historic Sites Restoration office. We bought windows and beadboard from Historic Albany's warehouse; using that material we repaired the walls and replaced half of the windows. We primed the walls and ceiling with white paint; we completed installation of the subflooring, and we reinstalled the original front step.

By the end of 2007, the school was in good condition structurally, and the shell was sound. During the summer of 2008, we finished replacing the windows (school and woodshed) and repaired a window sill; we replaced the exterior molding on the SE corner of the schoolhouse, repaired the woodshed door and button, and repaired the siding above the front door of the schoolhouse. We purchased period doors from Historic Albany Warehouse to replace the exterior and two interior doors, painted the interior walls, ceiling and molding, and installed new Douglas fir, tongue-and-groove flooring (the same kind of floor the schoolhouse had when it was last used as a school). Extra stone that was found inside the school along with salvaged hand-hewn beams were used to demarcate parking and display the beams. We painted and installed baseboards, installed blackboards (donated by Berne Knox Westerlo School) on the east and north walls, applied a coat of white opaque stain to the siding of both the schoolhouse and woodshed (the color when the building was last used as a school), moved furniture (including the restored desks) and the stove into the schoolhouse, and turned over the keys to Parks.

The students in the photo (from the late 1920's) are, from left to right, Marshall Warner, Beulah Ketcham and David Sagendorf. The photos show how much the restored classroom is like the original, and how similar the stoves are.

Parks created and installed three permanent displays in 2008-09 (two inside and one outside) in time for the Grand Opening on July 11, 2009. Finally, in 2010, the Friends of Thacher Park, with financial support from the Helderberg Kiwanis Club and the Knox Historical Society, purchased (and Parks installed) a historic marker for the school.

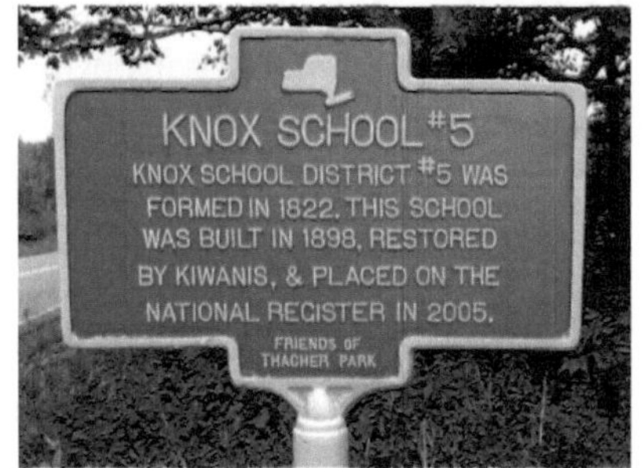

Additional newspaper articles, photos and more may be found on the Albany Hilltowns Wiki at: http://albanyhilltowns.com/wikiKnox/index.php?title=Knox_School_District_No._5.

9
References

Guide for Recording Quotations, by Maxine Lorang, Historic Cherry Hill; based on the Chicago Manual of Style, 13th edition, 1982

History of the County of Albany from 1609 to 1886, by George R. Howell and Jonathan Tenney; New York, 1886

Indian Ladder – A History of Life in the Helderbergs, by Gary L. Donhardt; Donhardt and Daughters Publishers, Collierville, TN, 2001

Knox, New York Sesquicentennial booklet; privately published in 1972; Frieda Saddlemire, Chair of the Publication Committee (republished in 2014 by the Knox Historical Society)

Landmarks of Albany County New York; Edited by Amasa J. Parker of Albany, NY; Published by D.Mason & Co., Syracuse, NY, 1897

Stone By Stone – The Magnificent History of New England's Stone Walls, by Robert M. Thorson; Walker & Company, New York, 2002

Tin Horns and Calico, by Henry Christman; Hope Farm Press, Cornwallville, NY, 1975

APPENDIX I

INTERVIEWS WITH FORMER STUDENTS AND USERS OF THE SCHOOLHOUSE

22 February 2002 – Videotaped interview with Pauline (Salisbury) Williman and Bill Salisbury. Betty Ketcham conducted this interview. Betty grew up on the adjacent farm and has known the Salisburys her whole life. During the interview they refer to several relatives by their first names. Bill and Pauline had sisters Grace and Loretta; their father and mother were Harrison and Alta. Pauline and Bill's great-grandfather, Jacob A. Hallenbeck is listed in the school board records beginning in 1830. Betty's father was Don (Donny); his sisters were Eleanor, Beulah and Edith, and his father was Egbert (Bert).

The Salisbury farm was about one-quarter mile east of the schoolhouse on the north side of Ketcham Road. Bill's home is just behind where the farmhouse stood. Before the Salisburys, Isaac Reamer owned the farm (Isaac Reamer was clerk of the school board beginning in 1865). Pauline and Bill are related to the Reamers through their grandmother.

Bill's first teacher was Edith Ketcham, Betty Ketcham's aunt; Edith got married while she was teaching. After Knox School #5, Bill went to Altamont to High School and graduated in 1944; his mother drove the schoolbus (their station wagon) to Altamont until about 1950. Alta also taught at the Berne School #5 on Beaver Dam Road, also known as the Helderberg School. Their youngest sister, Loretta, went to high school in Altamont for one year; when she tried to transfer to Berne-Knox they wouldn't accept her credits. School board members who presided over closing Knox #5 (and going into Berne-Knox) included Bert Ketcham (head of the school board) and Homer Corbin (who married Eleanor).

Two children who went to school with Bill and Pauline were Elva (Elvie) White and her sister (their parents were Hap and Ellen). Elvie was a scrappy one and used to push Bill in the creek. So one day, Pauline pushed Elvie into the creek; after that, she didn't push Bill anymore.

Suzie, Evelyn, Curt and Ada Secor also went to school there, as did Dave Sagendorf. Curt and Dave went to school with Pauline. The Secors lived in a house on Ryan Road behind the Salisbury farm.

In 1937, Bill was custodian at the school. He carried water to put in the cooler, started the fire in the stove, and swept out the mudroom. For that he was paid $10 for the year. He put the $10 in Albany Savings Bank, but never withdrew it. Miss Rivenburg was teacher at that timc.

Pauline began school in September 1930. During the spring before she started, the teacher, Miss Blake, invited Pauline to spend a day with her at the school. Miss Blake didn't return to school that year, so Pauline's first teacher was Ella (Schultes) Scrafford.

In May of 1930, Pauline was so sick that she had to go to City Hospital. She was upset that her mother didn't visit her there. Her father said that her mother wasn't feeling well; back then they didn't tell children when a new child was on the way. But on the way home from the hospital, they stopped at Memorial Hospital to pick up her mother and new baby Grace.

Pauline asked Bill if the cloakroom was on the left as you entered the building. Bill replied that as you entered, there was a mudroom divided from the classroom by a partition all the way across. He said that the cloakroom and some shelves for spare books were on the right at the entrance along with the "water fountain." He said that the stove was in the NW corner of the schoolroom (but when I interviewed him at the schoolhouse, he pointed to the SW corner).

The photo shows Pauline, Bill and the author at the Nature Center during the Grand Opening of the restored schoolhouse.

For a while during a bad winter, they couldn't get to the school because the roads were not plowed, and Edith held class in the Salisbury living room. The roads were only plowed sometimes; Elmer Van Duzen plowed them. One year their father bought Pauline and Bill sheepskin coats to use to walk to school. Very soon after that they had a minus 20-degree day. They asked their father if they could stay home, but he said that was why he bought them the coats. So they walked to school. No one else was there, so they walked home – but, their father said, at least they tried.

Bill explained that there was a woodshed across from the school door, and two outhouses to the right as you left the school. Pauline added that one day when she was using the girls' outhouse, some boys opened the door and made fun of her. As a result, she wouldn't go to the outhouse at school anymore. Her mother became suspicious when she would always have to use their outhouse before coming inside at the end of the day, so Pauline explained what happened. The next morning, her mother told another student, Beulah, who took care of the problem. Pauline said that they had to ask permission to go to the outhouse, and Bill added that when he was in school, they had to write their initials on the board so that only one would be out at a time.

Bill and Pauline estimated that there were from 7 to 12 students at the school – including four Secors; two Whites; two Salisburys; and Beulah Ketcham.

When Beulah went to high school in Altamont, Beulah's brother Don would pick her up after school in a car with a rumble seat. A few times Don let Pauline ride along in the rumble seat. Pauline was impressed, and she was also impressed with Ken Hallenbeck's convertible. (Pauline owned a convertible at the time of this interview.)

Teachers Bill or Pauline had in Knox School #5 were: Ella (Schultes) Scrafford from Berne, Pauline's first teacher; Venita Davis who boarded with the Salisburys for ½ year and married their cousin; Edith Ketcham; Miss Rivenburg who boarded with the Salisburys; and Mrs. Filkins of Rensselaerville whose husband drove her to school. Immediately before Ella Schultes was Miss Blake, and before her was Fanny Ellis; both Blake and Ellis boarded with the Salisburys. The teachers who boarded with them were just like family; they didn't take any special interest in Bill or Pauline.

Venita Davis was from Binghamton and was a singer. When she lived with the Salisburys, she had her piano shipped up, and would practice singing at night. Her favorite song was Ciribiribin which Pauline learned to dislike (until years later when she heard the Harry James version). At the beginning of the school day, she would have the students sing. During the singing, she walked around and stopped at every desk to listen; at Pauline's desk she would say "complete monotone," which made Pauline feel small.

Fanny Ellis was a wild driver; she drove her car up a phone pole one day. Also, while she lived with the Salisburys she dated a man who called himself Dean Davis. Mr. Salisbury was suspicious, and, after asking around about him, told Fanny that he thought that was not his real name and that he was actually married with a family. Fanny protested saying what a nice man he was, but on the next date she found out the Mr. Salisbury was correct and she never dated the man again.

Fanny Ellis finally married a man named Nadeau from Ticonderoga. Some years later (about 30 years before this interview), when Pauline was working up there at a public hearing on their water supply, she met a man named Edward Nadeau, a member of their board of supervisors. Pauline asked him about Fanny. It turned out that Fanny Ellis was his mother. He had been trying unsuccessfully to get information about her for years; so Pauline told him what she knew and sent him a picture of his mother.

Bill had to leave at about this point in the interview.

In the one-room schoolhouse, one teacher had to teach all grades and subjects. The day started with the pledge to the flag. When a subject was taught, the lesson was for everyone, even though some students may have known the topic already. The blackboard was on the left as you entered the classroom. The desks faced the blackboard; each had their own desk. When Pauline was there the students used paper, not slate tablets. They studied the standard Reading, Riting, and Rithmetic. Penmanship was important; they used the Palmer method. There was also a lot of emphasis on geography and history. Pauline feels she got a good education at the school. She wishes she knew what text books they used; her sister Loretta destroyed all their schoolbooks.

Pauline's mother, who taught at Berne School #5 on Beaver Dam Road across from Bush Drive, pushed Pauline along in school, so she graduated early. She went to high school in Altamont from where she graduated in 1940. She was so young that the other students ignored her except to ridicule the way she dressed. The families in Altamont were relatively well off financially; many worked for State government in Albany, so their children dressed differently than a poor farm girl from the Hill. Still, she has returned to many of her high school reunions.

During breaks in the schoolwork, they would occasionally walk up to Mrs. Horn's house for cookies. Mrs. Horn had no children, but made great German sugar cookies. She would give them cookies, and then Mr. Leonard Horn, with a smile, would threaten them saying "Now you go back to school or I press your pants for Sunday!"

The Horns lived in the first house west of the school on the north side of Ketcham Road. A man named Paul lived with them for a while before they passed away, and then he continued to live there for a while. After that Bill Secor owned the place, then Dick Edwards, and now New York State. One day on their way to Mrs. Horn's they saw a big pool of blood in the road. They reported it to their teacher Edith; the police were called, and the police asked them to stay in the schoolhouse. Finally the police reported that the dogcatcher had shot a stray dog, and the kids were allowed to go home.

The police were concerned because the area around Thompson's Lake was a hotbed of bootleg activity during Prohibition. Pauline remembers that the police were often out at night with searchlights looking for bootleggers. In fact, Mrs. Horn herself operated a still, for her own use; she had a reputation in the community.

A politician, Arthur Malloy had a large farm nearby where he had huge parties. Malloy let Pauline's dad, Harrison, grow grain and hay on his fields. One day Malloy's handyman showed Harrison the inside of the icehouse; it was loaded with booze. On the way out Malloy discovered them. About a week later the handyman was found dead; it was ruled a suicide. Pauline thinks that her father was lucky.

Dan O'Connell, Tommy Hayden of East Berne, and others were also involved in rooster fights. The Salisburys were occasionally paid to board the roosters. At the time, the kids didn't understand why people wanted them to board roosters

Pauline's Grandfather Hallenbeck lived on Beaver Dam Road near Dan O'Connell's place. The O'Connells bought their place from her grandfather. He may also have sold some property to Camp Pinnacle.

9 June 2003 – Videotaped interview with Bill Salisbury at the schoolhouse. Bill started school in 1932 when he was five years old. He graduated from the school in 1939, the last year the school was used. Pauline finished at Knox No. 5 in 1936 when she was 10. She went to high school in Altamont and graduated in 1940 when she was 14; she then had to wait 2 years until she was old enough to get into business school. After the school was closed, a relative of Dick Edwards, the owner, lived in the building for two or three summers. Later, the building was used by the Helleberg Coon Club; Earl Wagoner was president of the club, and Dick Monroe and Ernie Walk were two of its members.

Bill was school custodian in 1937; he was paid $10 for the year. He carried drinking water to the school in the morning, started the stove and swept out the mudroom. The stove was in the corner and hooked to the chimney; the chimney is in the same location today (in the middle of the west side on the outside of the building). Bill pointed to show that the stove was in the corner of the schoolhouse on the same end as the chimney and away from the road (the SW corner). Neighbors cut wood for the stove from the woods behind the schoolhouse and piled it in the woodshed. Bill carried wood from the woodshed to the school; it was piled in the mudroom to the left of the entrance. The mudroom is also where the coats, lunches and water were kept. Bill climbed the apple tree to the right of the woodshed a good many times. The maple tree to the left of the woodshed was about half the size it is now.

The school was painted white. He thinks that they installed electricity in the school during the last year or two that he was there.

The roof was made of wooden shingles; the Coon club probably put on the present metal roof. The outside of the school is much the same now as when Bill went there. The concrete foundation along the south side of the school is probably not original; the original was stone. He is not aware that the school was ever in another location.

The woodshed roof has the original wooden shingles. The woodshed had a wooden door with a handle that they called a "button." The button was a stick of wood with a nail; it was fastened to the doorframe and was turned to open the door. The woodshed was not locked. The schoolhouse had a regular knob and was locked.

Bill's father cultivated the field behind the woodshed (to the east). He had a dairy farm with barn-room for thirty-three cows, a big herd at the time.

The outhouses, to the right as you exited the schoolhouse, were not quite to the edge of the woods. The girls' outhouse was on the right, the boys' on the left with an alleyway between them. To go to the outhouse, students had to write their initials on the blackboard so that boys and girls would not be out at the same time.

His teachers were Edith Ketcham, [Venita Davis], Miss [Mabel] Rivenburg and Mrs. Filkins from Rensselaerville. Most of the teachers boarded with the Salisburys in their home which stood in front of Bill's current home. The teacher's desk was in the middle of the right wall (the wall closest to the road. The student desks could be pushed around; they were not attached to the floor. The blackboard was on the left partition as you entered the classroom.

Only 5 or 6 students typically attended the school at any time; the maximum might be 10 or 12. I asked Bill who some of the other students were. He remembered Suzie (Secor) Livingston, who now lives in New Salem; Dave Sagendorf, who Bill incorrectly thought was dead; and the Warner children. The Warner children came to school in a horse and buggy; their house was behind where Bill now lives, on land now owned by Pauline. There is also a 200-year-old house behind Bill's house on land now owned by the State.

The mention of the Warner children in the previous paragraph seemed to conflict with Bill's earlier interview with Betty Ketcham. So I asked Bill about it one day while he was working at the Knox Transfer Station. He agreed that the children were the Whites. [Pauline added that the youngest was Elva and the other may have been Bernice; their parents were Hap and Ellen White.] The two girls were the grandchildren of Byron Warner, and it was probably his son Marshall Warner who drove the horse and buggy.

Students could progress at their own pace by taking test papers; they could advance more than one grade in a year if they had the ability. Bill recalls that during recess, some of the students built a little village out in the woods behind the school. They built it out of little logs; the buildings were small, not even the size of a big birdhouse. Another thing they did during recess was visit something like a little cave about ¼ to ½ mile back in the woods behind the school. It was open on both ends, and there was always ice inside.

Bill recalled that old Dr. Brenenstuhl used to visit the school to examine the students. He told the kids how bad it was for them to eat candy, and then he gave them a candy bar as he left.

18 June 2003 – I spoke with Mrs. Isabelle (Quay) Baker by phone. She declined to be interviewed on videotape and asked that her name not be put in any newspaper.

She was 90 years old at the time of the interview and went to school at Knox School No. 5 beginning in about 1920; she went to high school in Altamont. Don Ketcham went to Knox School No. 5 with her. Don's father used to drive them to school on a sleigh in bad weather, but they had to walk home with the wind at their back. She lived down the hill from Ketcham's farm on the right, near where she now lives (the house she and her husband Walter built; he is deceased). [According to Pauline Williman, Isabelle's parents were Clarence and Alta Quay.] Walter was Knox Town Supervisor for one term; he ran again but lost.

She knew Dave and Christina Sagendorf. Mrs. Milner helped take care of Dave when he went into the nursing home.

The woodshed was enlarged when she was at the school, but she doesn't remember any work being done on the school itself; it is the same now as when she was in school.

She remembers two games they played at recess: Ducky-on-the-Rock (a small stone was placed on a larger stone; they tried to knock the small stone off by throwing other stones at it); and Anti-Over (they stood on both sides of the schoolhouse and threw stones over the roof; if they caught a stone they ran to the other side to tag the person).

There was a pond near the school. They would walk to the pond to try to find frogs, which they would put in a jar with holes in the lid and take back to the school.

The school had a potbelly stove; she remembered it being roughly in the center of the room. The room also had a blackboard, and benches and desks on one side. In the anteroom where they hung their coats, there was a bucket of drinking water that they drank from a dipper.

24 June 2003 – Interview with Suzie (Secor) Livingston at her home in New Salem. Marion Parmenter, the Vice-president of the New Scotland Historical Association participated in the interview. Suzie was born in 1925 and started school at "the little school," near the corner of Old Stage Road and Thompson's Lake Road, in 1931 or 1932. She transferred to Knox School No. 5 in about 1935. They lived on Ryan Road "up in the back where Ray Williman now lives." [According to Pauline Williman, Don and Margaret Ketcham lived in the house where Susie lived, after they were married and before Ray and Melva Williman moved in.] Later, in about 1937, she went to Berne-Knox because they moved to Long Road.

I asked her about games they played at recess. She recalled Ducky-on-the-Rock in which kids had to jump on rocks to be "safe." She recalled Anti-Over in which the kids threw a ball over the schoolhouse roof; if a person did not catch the ball, they were "out." They also played Fox-and-Geese when there was snow on the ground;

they would make a large circle in the snow with lines; they were "safe" in the center. They also played Hopscotch and Jump-Rope. There was also a pond near the school where they would ice skate after school. It wasn't much of a pond; in summer the pond would dry up.

While she went to Knox School No. 5 there was one other student in her class and eight or so in the school. Students did a lot of reading. There was no time limit on the tests; she recalls that they had tests in arithmetic and maybe history.

The outside of the school was white. As you entered the schoolhouse, the firewood and water were on the left; they used a dipper in the bucket to drink the water. The coatroom was near the firewood; they probably had nails on which to hang their coats. Entering the classroom, the teacher's desk was on the right. The blackboard was on the other side of the doorway. The stove was in the back corner, on the far left as you entered. I mentioned that there was a small room around the partition to the right; she thought it might have been used for supplies. There was a ceiling in the school, and the floors were hardwood.

Suzie said that her younger sisters Evelyn and Ada, and her brother Curtis also went to school at Knox No. 5. Curtis hung out with Dave Sagendorf. It took them about an hour to walk to school because the youngest sister was only 5 or 6 years old. Edith Ketcham, Donny Ketcham's sister, was one of her teachers.

24 June 2003 – Bedside interview with David Sagendorf. Dave had been a student at the Knox School #5 and lived on Ketcham Road all his life. At the time of the interview, he was in the hospice wing of the Daughters of Sarah Nursing Home. I introduced myself and told him that Pauline (Salisbury) Williman asked me to say hello to him; he remembered Pauline and Bill. I said that the Kiwanis Club was interested in fixing up the schoolhouse.

He recalls that the school and woodshed were painted white. I showed him a picture of the woodshed; he said that it was built about the time he started school - he recalls when the school stood there by itself. I asked him what years he went to school there. He answered that he was born in 1916 and is now 83. [His neighbor on Ketcham Road, Marty Milner, confirmed that Dave was actually born about 1920 (2003 minus 83).] So he probably attended the school from about 1926 to about 1936; he recalls getting out of school in the 1930's when he was 16. He worked on the farm until he got married, and then went into construction work. [So the woodshed was probably built around 1926.]

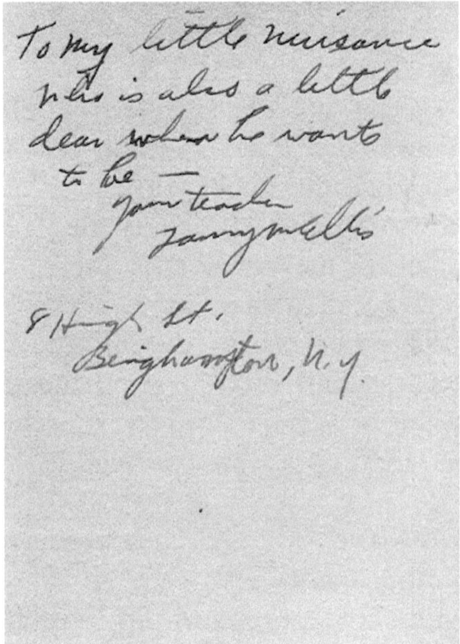

The photo above (both front and back) was given to Dave by his teacher Fanny Ellis.

I showed him a picture of the schoolhouse viewed from the southwest; he mentioned that the chimney on the schoolhouse was oriented differently when he was there – "the chimney was headed up this way instead of down that way." He apparently thought he was looking at a different view and thought the chimney should be on the other end. I showed him a view of the schoolhouse entrance and he remembered that the entrance headed toward the Salisbury farm.

Marty Milner has some of the schoolbooks used at the school; they belonged to Bill. Bill said that they are now Marty's and he can do anything he wants with them.

When I explained that the Kiwanis was going to restore the schoolhouse, he responded that "it ain't got nothing to do with me no more." "I don't want to know nothing about that school no more; I don't even want to hear about it now. I hated it."

10 July 2003 - Telephone interview with Earl Wagoner, former president of the Helleberg Coon Club. The Coon Club used the schoolhouse for 12 to 15 years. I asked Earl what year the Coon Club had begun using the building. He didn't remember, but he said that the Club was incorporated as The Helleberg Coon Club, Inc. in 1976; they had 20 to 25 members. During the time they used the building they installed electricity, replaced some of the siding, replaced some of the 2x6-inch floor joists, replaced some of the sills with long railroad ties, and did some foundation work (including, probably, the poured concrete on the south side of the building). They used the building for meetings, dinners, and the sale of pelts.

Finally, the owner of the property, Dick Edwards, asked the club to leave so that a relative of his could live in the building. The relative stayed for only a few weeks, but the Coon Club never used the building again.

APPENDIX II

TRANSCRIPT OF THE RECORDS OF SCHOOL DISTRICT NO. 5 IN THE TOWN OF KNOX

(Transcribed by Daniel A. Driscoll)

Front Cover:
[Records?] of District
School District No.5 in the
Town of Knox
1st January, 1831 --

Inside Front Cover:
Records of
School District No.5 in the
Town of Knox

Thomas Stafford Clerk
1st January, 1831 --
[The following was added in a different handwriting:]
School Dist.
No.5 in the Town
of Knox John M Williams, Jr.

[The following was in pencil on a separate page.]

		feet in
Sloan wood first Load,		96.00
Second	do,	112.00

[The following was written upside down:]
Toal at the first gate .2.2.1
Second gate 1.2.2.2

[1824 October]

At an annual meeting of the freeholders and inhabitants of School District No.5 conveined at the School house in Said district agreeable to legal notice John Stafford chosen chairman and Jacob P. Mesick Sect. of Said meeting. Resolved that Simon Secor John J. Levingston

At an annual meeting of the freeholders and
inhabitants of School District No 5 Convened at
the School house in Said district agreeable to legal
notice John Stafford chosen Chairman and Jacob P.
Mesick Secty of Said meeting, Resolved that Simon
Sacer John J. Levingston and Nicholas Brunk
be trustees. and Jacob P. Mesick Clerk and
John Tygert Collector for the insuing Year
Resolved that there be a tax levied on the inhab-
-itants of Said District of five Dollars for
repairing the School house, Resolved that the
next annual meeting be on the last Saturday
in October next by adjournment, Dated
at School District No 5 in the town of
Knox this 2d October A.D. 1824

Jacob P. Mesick Clerk

1825 May } Nicholas Brunk one of the trustees of
School District No 5 in the town of Knox
Received public money from the Commission-
-ers of Said town which was $35 - 52 cents
paid to Helem Mead District teacher
as appears from Receips of trustees

Jacob P. Mesick Clerk

and Nicholas Brunk be trustees. and Jacob P. Mesick Clerk and John Tygert Collector for the insuing Year

Resolved that there be a tax levied on the inhabitants of Said District of five Dollars for repairing the School house, Resolved that the next annual meeting be on the last Saturday in October next by adjournment, Dated at School District No.5 in the town of Knox this 2th October A.D. 1824

Jacob P. Mesick Clerk

1825 May

Nicholas Brunk one of the trustees of School District No. 5 in the town of Knox Received public money from the Commissioner of Said town which was $35..52 cents paid to Helem [sic] Mead District teacher as appears from Receipts of trustees -

Jacob P. Mesick Clerk

1825 [December]

At an annual meeting of the freeholders and inhabitants of School District No.5 conveined at the School house in Said District agreeable to legal notice John Stafford chosen Chairman and Jacob P. Mesick Sect Resolved that Peter B. Winney John J. Levingston and John Stafford be trustees for the insuing year Jacob P. Mesic clerk & John Tygert Collector

Resolved that there be a tax of five Dollars levied on the inhabitants of Said District for the purpose of repairing the School house,- Resolved that the next Annual meeting be on the last Saturday in October next at two oclock P.M.-Knox 11 Dec. 1825-

1826 April

John Levingston one of the trustees of School District No.5 in the town of Knox Received public money from the Commissioners of Common Schools of Said town the amount of which was $34..82 Jacob P. Mesick Clerk –

and paid $15=00 of the same to [Helim?] Mead teacher as appears by his receipt dated April 22nd 1826

1826 [October]

At an annual meeting of the freeholders and inhabitants of the School district No.5 convened at the School house in Said district agreeable to Legal notice Isaac Stafford chosen Chairman and John Levingston Sect. of Said meeting,. Resolved that Amos Whipple Mathew Van= =Alstine ["Van" is at the end of one line followed by the "=" sign; "Alstine" is at the beginning of the next line preceded by an "=" sign.] and Wilhelmas Pier be the trustees Jacob P Mesick district Clerk and Henry Cornelius Collector for the insuing year, Resolved that the next annual meeting be on the first Saturday in October next at the School house in Said district at two oclock in the afternoon by adjournment, Dated at School district No.5 in the town of Knox this 28th October A.D. 1826

1827 April

Wilhelmas Pier one of the trustees of School District No.5 in the town of Knox received public money from the Commissioners of common School of Said town the amount of which was $[ ]

Jacob P. Mesick Clerk

1827 [October]

At an annual meeting of the freeholders and inhabitants of School District No.5 conveined at at [sic] the School house in Said District agreeable to legal notice Isaac Stafford chosen chairman and Jacob P. Mesick Sect. of Said meeting, [Instead of a period after the abbreviations "Sect." and "No." the writer uses a dash under the last letter with two dots under the dash.] Resolved that Nicholas Brunk John Levingston and Peter B. Winney be trustees for the insueing [sic] year. Jacob P. Mesick Clerk and Isaac Stafford collector; Resolved that the next annual meeting be on the first Saturday in november next at the School house at two oclock in the afternoon by adjournment, Dated at School district no.5 in the town of Knox this 7th October A.D. 1827

1828 April

Nicholas Brunk one of the trustees of School district No.5 in the town of Knox Received public money from the Commissioners [The double "s" was written as in Germany, looking similar to the script "fs."] of Common Schools of Said town the amount of which was $34..41 and paid the Same to Alpheus Persons teacher as appears from Record, - Jacob P. Mesick Clerk

1828 [November]

At an annual meeting of the freeholders and inhabitants of School District No.5 in the town of Knox conviened at the School house in Said District according to legal notice. Nicholas Brunk chosen chairman and Jacob P. Mesick Sect. of Said meeting Resolved that Isaac Hungerford Nicholas Brunk and John Levingston be the trustees Jacob P Mesick District Clerk and Isaac Stafford Collector for the insuing year, - Resolved that the the [sic] next annual meeting be on the first Saturday of november next at the School house in Said district at two oclock in the afternoon by adjournment, - Dated at School District No.5 in the town of Knox this 1st November 1828 -

1829 march

Nicholas Brunk one of the trustees of School District No.5 in the town of Knox Received public money from the Commissioners of Common Schools of Said town the amount of which was $29..48 paid the Same to Hezekiah Reynolds & Tyler - teachers, as appears from his Receipts from Said teachers

Receipt from Datus E. Tyler -------- $15..00
Receipt from Hezekiah Reynolds --- $14..50
$29..50

Jacob P. Mesiek.-Clerk

1829 7th Nov.

At an annual meeting of the inhabitants of School District No.5 in the town of Knox Conveined at the School house in Said District agreeable to legal notice, Resolved that Peter Pitcher be chairman and Jacob P. Mesick Sect. of Said meeting,-

Resolved that Isaac Hungerford. Peter B. Winney and Thomas Stafford, be the trustees for the insuing year. Jacob P. Mesick district clerk and Henry P. Mesick Collector, Resolved that the district School house Shall not be used for the purpose of Singing School for the term of one year from the above date, Resolved that there be a tax of Six Dollars levied on the taxable inhabitants of this School District for the purpose of repairing the School house [&?] Resolved that all the public money Recd. from the Commissioners of Said town Shall be paid to the teacher as Soon as it is Recd. if it Shall be then due to any teacher,-

Resolved that the next annual meeting be on the last Saturday of november next at the School house at two oclock in the afternoon,- Dated at School district No.5 in the town of Knox this 7th November 1829 -

Jacob P. Mesick dist. clk

[1830 January]

[This report was close to the back of the book.]

1830

To the Commissioners of Common Schools of the town of Knox and County of albany we the trustees of school district No. 5 in said town in conformity with the Statute for the Support of Common Schools do certify and report that the whole time any school has been kept in our district during the year ending on the date here of and since the date of the last report for said district is ten months and six days and that the time during said year and since said last report, our school, has been kept by teachers duly appointed and approved in all respects according to law, [The thought appears to have been interrupted at this point, and the ink becomes slightly lighter.] that the amount of money received in our district from the Commissioners of Common Schools during the Said year and since the date of the said last report is twenty nine dollars and forty eight cents, and that the same has been expended in paying the teachers wages. that the number of children taught in said district during said year and since said last report is fifty eight and that the number of children residing in our district on the first day of January inst. who are over five and under sixteen years of

[next page]

age is seventy four and that the names of the parents or other persons with whom such children respectively reside and the number residing with each are as follows

Parents	Children
Peter B. Winney	5
Seamour Swan	3
Matthias Reamer	3
Jacob A. Hallenbec	3
Wm. Swan	1
George F Hart	1
Ormond Stafford	2
Nicholas Brunk	3
Nicholas N. Smith	2
Joseph [Phlipsey?]	1
Wms. Pitcher	4
George Pitcher	1
Wms. Pier	3
	32

Parents	Children
Francis Hurst	5
Wm. Tygart	2
Wm. Dennis	1
Isaac Hungerford	2
Isaac Stafford	3
Peter Pitcher	3
Sarah Livingston. wd.	3
Henry Toles	3
Simon Secor	6
Andrew Secor Jr.	8
Jacob P. Mesick	2
Jeremiah Pitcher	1
Henry Hurst	3
	42

And we further report that our School has been visited by the inspectors of Common Schools twice during the year preceding this report and

[next page]

that the Sum paid for teachers wages over and above the public money apportioned to said district during the Same year amounts to fifty four dollars and ninety one Cents.

Dated at Knox this first day of January in the year of our lord one thousand eight hundred and thirty

Thomas Stafford }
Peter B. Winney } Trustees
Isaac Hungerford }

1830 march

Thomas Stafford one of the trustees of School District No.5 in the town of Knox, Received public money from the commissioners of common Schools of Said town the amount of which was $30..80 ct. and paid the Same to Hezehiah Reynolds teacher in Said District as appears by his receipt Dated 19th march 1830

1830 27th Nov.

At an anual [sic] meeting of the freeholders and inhabitants of School District No.5 in the town of Knox conveined at the school house in said District agreeable to legal notice, Resolved that Simon Secor be chairman and Thomas Stafford Sect. of said meeting -

Resolved that Jacob P. Mesick Simon Secor and Peter B. Winney be the trustees for the ensuing year Thomas Stafford district Clerk and Isaac Hungerford Collector, Resolved that the public money be paid out in two equal payments one half for the winter school and the other half for the summer School, Resolved that the next annual meeting be held at the school house the last Saturday in October next at 2 oclock P.M. Dated at school district No.5 in the town of Knox this 27th of Nov. 1830

Thomas Stafford dist. Clk

1831 April

Jacob P. Mesik one of the trustees of school District No.5 in the town of Knox received public money of the Commissioners of Common schools of said town the amount of which was $25=97

Thomas Stafford. Clerk

1831

The above amount paid to Henry Ogsberry teacher as appears by report-

T. Stafford. Clk.

1831 29th Oct.

At an annual meeting of the freeholders and inhabitants of school District Number five in the town of Knox Convened at the school house in said district agreeable to legal notice -

Resolved that Isaac Hungerford be Chairman and Thomas Stafford sect. of said meeting -

Resolved that Matthias Brunk, 2nd Jacob P. Mesick and Wilhelmas Pitcher be the Trustees for the insuing year Thomas Stafford Clerk and Isaac Hungerford Collector

Resolved that the next annual meeting be on the last Saturday in October next at 2 oclock in the P.M. by adjournment Dated at School District No.5 in the town of Knox this 29th of October 1831

Thomas Stafford Clerk

[1832 January]

To the Commissioners of Common Schools of the Town of Knox, We the trustees of School district No.5 in Said town in conformity with the Statute for the Support of common Schools do certify and report that the whole time any School has been kept in our district, during the Year ending on the date hereof, and Since the date of the last report for Said district is Seven months & thirteen days and that the time during Said Year and Since Said last report Such School has been kept by a teacher duly appointed and approved in all respects according to law is three months, that the amount of money Received in our district from the Commissioners of Common Schools during the Said Year and Since the date of the Said last report is twenty five dollars & ninty seven cents and that the Said Sum has been applied to the payment of the compensation of teachers employed in Said district & qualified as the Statute prescribes, that the number of children taught in Said district during Said Year and Since Said last report is fifty two, and that the No. of children residing in our district on the last day of December last, who are over five, & under Sixteen years of Age is fifty Six and that the names of the parents, or other persons with whom Such Children respectively reside, and the No. residing with each, are as follows, viz.

parents	No. of children
Andrew Secor [Jun?]	7
Henry Toler	1
Mathias Brunk	2
Sarah Levingston	3
Peter B. Winne	5
Jacob P. Mesick	3
Isaac Hungerford	3
Nicholas Brunk	4
William Tygert	1
Jeremiah Pitcher	2
Simon Secor	5
Isaac Stafford	3
Armond Stafford	3
Seymour Swan	3
Jacob Helenbake	3
Wilhelmas Pitcher	3

Henry Cornelius	2
William Denis	2
Leonard Schermerhorn	1
Total	56

next page -----

and we further report that our School has not been inspected at all by any of the inspectors of Common Schools, and that the Sum paid for teachers wages over & above the public moneys apportioned to Said district during the Same year amounts to nineteen dollars & twelve cents –

Dated at Knox this 1st day January 1832 –

[The above report appears to be in Jacob P. Mesick's handwriting.]

1832 April

Jacob P. Mesick one of the trustes of common Schools in District Number five in the town of Knox received public money of the Commissioners of Common Schools in Said town the amount of which was $20-6cts. T.Stafford Clk.

The above twenty Dollars & Six cents Received by Jacob P. Mesick one of the trustees of School District No.5 in the town of Knox in April last was paid out to the District teacher as will appear by the following Receipt. - Received of Jacob P. Mesick & Mathias Brunk trustees of School District No.5 in the town of Knox twenty dollars & Six cents public money for teaching School in Said District Said term ending 27th October 1832 -

Jacob P. Mesick Clerk - Hezekiah Reynolds

1832 [October]

At an annual meeting of the Inhabitants of School District No.5 in the town of Knox conveined at the School house in Said District agreeable to legal notice,- resolved that Nicholas Brunk be Chairman and Isaac Hungerford Sect. of Said meeting -

Resolved that Nicholas Brunk Simon Secor and Isaac Hungerford be the trustees for the insuing Year Jacob P. Mesick District Clerk & Mathias Brunk Collector, - Resolved that there be a tax levied of fifty Dollars on the taxable inhabitants of Said District for the purpose of takeing down moveing & rebuilding the School house in Said District.- Resolved that the Site for Said School house be on the public highway or near the Same Called the newroad on the line between Simon Secor and Isaac Hungerford a northerly Course from where it now Stands about five hundred Yards Resolved that the next annual meeting be on the last Saturday in October next at three oclock P.M. at the School house in Said District by adjournment Dated At School District No.5 in the town of Knox this 27th October 1832.-

Jacob P. Mesick Dist. Clerk

April 1833

Simon Secor one of the trustees of School District No.5 in the town of Knox Received public money from the Commissioners of common Schools of Said town the amount of which was. viz $18.46. April 22nd. 1833.- Jacob P. Mesick Clerk

1834 [October]

At an anual meeting of the inhabitants of School District No.5. in the town of Knox held at the school house in [said?] District on the 25th October 1834 Resolved that Peter B. Winne Nicholas Brunk and Henry Cornelius be the trustees and Isaac Hungerford Clerk. Resolved that Jacob Brunk be the collector of said District Resolved that the site of the school house be at or near the house of Isaac Ostrander in said District Resolved that the next anual meeting be on the last Saturday in October next at 2 oclock P.M. at the school house in said District by adjournment Dated at school District No.5. in the town of Knox this 25th Oct 1834

Isaac Hungerford Clerk

1835 [October]

At an anual meeting of the inhabitants of School District No.5 in the town of Knox held at the school house in said District on the 30th October 1835 Resolved that Jacob Brunk Willhelmus Pitcher John McWilliams be the trustees and Isaac Hungerford Clerk Resolved that Storm Flansburg collector Resolved that the next anual meeting be on the last Saturday in October next at early candle light Dated at the school District No.5 in the town of Knox Isaac Hungerford Clerk

[1836 April]

[The following receipt was written on a page near the back of the book.]

1836. Jacob Brunk one of the trustees of School District Number 5. in the town of Knox Received the public money from the Commissioners of Common Schools in Said town the Amount of which was $18..

$18.. Dated at School District No. 5. in the town of Knox this 15th day of April 1836,

Isaac Hungerford Dist Clk

[1836 July]

At a Special meeting of the inhabitants of School district No.5 in the town of Knox convened at the house of Jacob A. Hellenbeck in Said District on the Second day of July 1836. by order of the trustees of Said district and agreeable to legal notice given by the Clerk of Said District.

Resolved that Nicholas Brunk be Chaiman of Said meeting and Isaac Hungerford Sect.

Resolved that the Site for Said District School house be on the land of Jacob A. Hellenbeck lying about twenty rods north from a bridge near Said Hellenbecks on road District [Ws.?] on the west side of Said road.

Resolved that the School house formerly belonging to Said district No.5 be moved on the Site hereby in the above Resilution [sic] designated as the Site for Said District School house

Resolved. that the tax of fifty dollars voted for at the last annual meeting in Said District be collected for the purpose of rebuilding Said District School house, The above resilutions were all passed and voted for by a majority of the whole present at the meeting, Dated at School district No.5 in the town of Knox this 2nd day of July 1836,

Nicholas Brunk - Chairman

Isaac Hungerford Secretary

1836 [November]

At an anual meeting of the inhabitants of school District No.5 in the town of Knox held at the school house in said District on the 5th November 1836 Resolved that Nicholas Brunk Storm Flansburg and Jacob P. Mesick be the trustees and Isaac Hungerford Clerk Resolved that Jacob Brunk be the collector of said District ~~Resolved the next anual meeting be on the first Saturday in November next at 2 oclock P.M. at the school house~~ [This resolution was crossed-out.]

continued
[next page]
1836 Continued

Resolved that there be a tax of fifty dollars levied on the taxable inhabitants of this school District for the purpose of rebuilding the school house, Resolved that the next anual meeting be on the first Saturday in November next at 2 oclock P.M. at the school house in said District, dated at school District No.5 in the town of Knox this 5th day of November 1836 Isaac Hungerford Clerk

[1836 December]

Received of Nicholas Brunk one of the trustees of School District No.5 in the town of Knox thirteen dollars and fifty cents being in full for work done on the School house in Said District. -

As Witness my hand this 22nd December 1836,

(Copy of Receipt) Henry G. Van Zandt

Isaac Hungerford, District Clerk

[In addition, the following receipt was written on the last page of the book.]

Received of the trustees of School District No. 5. in the town of Knox thirteen Dollars and fifty cents being in full up to this date, Dated 22nd Dec. [1836?]

(Copy of receipt) H. G. Van Zandt

[1837 February 1]

To the clerk of School District number 5 in the town of Knox, The trustees of District No.5 in Said town at a meeting held for the purpose, have resolved that a Special meeting be called at the School house on Saturday the 11th day of Feb inst. at 5 oclock P.M. of that day for the purpose of ascertaining the expence of building Said School house & the sum necessary to be raised to defray Said expences, and for the transaction of such other business as the meeting may deem necessary, You will therefore notify each taxable inhabitant of the district by reading this notice in his hearing or if he is absent from home by leaving a copy of [it or?] so much as Relates to the time & place of meeting, at the place of his abode at least five days before such meeting,-

Dated at School District No.5 in the town of Knox this first day of Feb. 1837.

(A Copy) Jacob P. Mesick \
Nicholas Brunk }trustees
Storm Flansburgh /
Isaac Hungerford District Clerk

[1837 February 11]

At a Special Meeting of the freeholders and inhabitants of School District No.5 in the town of Knox convened at the School house in Said district on the eleventh day of February 1837. by order of the trustees of Said district and agreeable to legal notice given by the clerk of Said district, Resolved that Nicholas Brunk be chairman of Said meeting and Isaac Hungerford Secretary,

Resolved that Said meeting be adjourned intill [sic] Saturday the 18th instant at 5 oclock P.M. at the School house in Said district (on motion of David Schermerhorn

Dated at School District No.5 in the town of Knox this Eleventh day of February 1837.

{Nicholas Brunk Chairman}
{Isaac Hungerford Clerk, }

[1837 February 18]

At a Special meeting of the freeholders & inhabitants of School District No.5 in the town of Knox convened at the School house in Said district on the 18th day of February 1837 pursuant to the above adjournment.

Resolved that Nicholas Brunk be chairman of Said meeting and Storm Flansburgh Secretary of Said meeting

Resolved that there be a tax of fifty dollars levied on the taxable inhabitants of Said District together with two dollars and fifty cents for collectors fees

Resolved that Said tax when collected be expended in defraying the expenses of building the School house in Said

[next page]

District, Resolved that all the money advanced by any of the inhabitants in Said District in building Said School house for materials and paying for [hier?] Shall be first paid out of the Said fifty dollars, and the residue to be paid to the Several creditors of Said district in proportion to the amount of their Several demands if it Should fall Short of paying their whole demands

Resolved that the residue of the demands of Said creditors if any Should be, Shall hereafter be collected by a tax to be levied for that purpose on the inhabitants of Said District

Resolved that the Accounts of the Creditors of Said district Shall be Audited by the trustees of Said District or a majority of Said trustees at a meeting to be held by Said trustees for that purpose so Soon as may be after the above Sum of fifty two dollars and fifty cents Shall be collected & returns made by Said Collector to the trustees of Said District,---

Dated at School District No.5 in the town of Knox the 18th day of February. 1837,

Nicholas Brunk - Chairman
Storm Flansburgh Secretary

[1837 February 25]

List of taxes payable by the following persons taxable inhabitants of School District number 5 in the town of Knox made by the trustees of Said District on the 25th day of February 1837 in conformlty to law.-

Names	Valuation of Real Estate	Personal Estate	Total	Amount of taxes
Jacob P. Mesick	$..760	..	..760	$4..13 cents
Jacob Brunk	..750	..	..750	..4..09
Jacob A. Hellenbeck	..400	..	..400	..2..13
Henry Cornelius	..400	..	..400	..2..13
Wilhelmas Pitcher	..860	..	..860	..4..70
William Tygert	..1025	..	..1025	..5..63
Francis Hurst	..500	..	..500	..2..72
Wilhelmas Pier	..420	..	..420	..2..30
Storm Flansburgh	..210	..	..210	..1..14
Isaac Hungerford	.1050	..	.1050	..5..73
Elias Stafford	.. .56	..	.. .56	..0..36
Sarah Stafford wd.	..135	..	..135	.0..73

Simon Secor	.1280	..200	1480	8..33
Leonard Schermehorn	..850	..	..850	4..65
David Schermehorn	.. ..	..200	..200	1..08
John Mc Williams	500	.. - -	..500	2..65
County of Albany [Ls,?]			Total	$52..50 amount

[next page]

To the Collector of School District number five in the town of Knox in the County Aforesaid Greeting. In the name of the people of the State of NEW York you are hereby commanded and required to collect from each of the inhabitants in the Annexed tax list or rate bill named the Sum of money Set opposite to his or her name in Said list and within thirty days after receiving this warrant to pay the Amount thereof Collected by you (retaining five per cent for your fees) into the hands of the trustees of Said district or Some or one of them and take his or their receipt therefore, And if Any of the Said inhabitants Shall not pay Such Sum on demand You are hereby further Commanded to levy the Same of his or her goods & chattels together with the costs and charges of Such levy & Sale in the Same manner as on Executions issued by a Justice of the peace,-

Given under our hands and Seals this 25th day of February 1837

Jacob P. Mesick. L.S. \
Nicholas Brunk L.S. }trustees
(A Copy) Storm Flansburgh . L.S./

[1837 November]

At a Special [sic] meeting of the freeholders and inhabitants of School District No.5 in the town of Knox convened at the School house in Said district on the 27th day of November 1837. by order of the trustees of Said district & agreeable to legal notice given by the Clerk of Said district for the purpose of Electing district officers in Said - District and the transaction of other business as the meeting may deem proper,

Resolved that Nicholas Brunk be Chairman of Said meeting and Isaac Hungerford Sect. -

Resolved that Derrick Van.Schaack. John.B.Winne and John Mc.Williams, be trustees, and Jacob P. Mesick Clerk. for the Insuing

Year & Jacob Brunk collector,- Resolved that the next Annual meeting be on the last Saturday in October next At 2.P.M. by adjournment,- Dated at School district No.5 in the town of Knox this 27th day of november 1837

Nicholas Brunk. Chairman }
Isaac Hungerford Sect.- }

[1839 January]

To the Commissioners of Common Schools of the town of Knox

We the trustees of School district No.5 formed partly out of the said town, and partly out of the adjoining town of New Scotland, do in conformity with the Statute for the Support of common Schools. certify and report.-

That the whole time any school has been kept in our district during the Year ending on the date hereof, and Since the date of the last report for said district is eight months and that the time during Said Year and Since Said last report. Such School has been kept by teachers after obtaining a certificate of qualification from the inspectors of common Schools is Eight months, that the total amount of money received by said district. from the Commissioners of Common Schools of the respective towns out of which said district is formed Since the date of the last annual report of said district, is eighteen dollars and twenty cents.-

And that the said sum has been applied to the payment of the compensation of teachers employed in said district and – qualifyed [sic] as the Statute prescribes, That the number of children taught in Said district during Said Year and Since Said last report. is Forty five, And that the number of children residing in our district on the last day of december last, who are over five and under Sixteen years of age,-

[next page]

is Fifty Six and that the names of the parents or other persons with whom Such children respectively reside and the number residing with each are as follows Viz. –

Parents names	No of children, -	Parents names	No. of children
John B. Winne	--4	Isaac Hungerford	--6
Jacob P.Mesick	--4	William Tygert	--1
William Dennis	--3	Storm Flansburgh	--2
Jacob Brunk	--3	Wilhelmas Pier	--4

John Reamer	--4	Francis Hurst	--2
John Mc Williams	--4	Derrick Van Schaack	--3
Henry Cornelius	--2	William Secor	--1
Casper Daget	--5	William Tygert [Jun?]	3
Aaron C. Hellenbeck	5		22
	34		34
		No.	56

And we do further Specify and report, that of the Said Sum of money so as above Stated to have been received in our Said district the Sum of Seventeen Dollars and Sixteen Cents was received for and on Account of that part of Said district lying in the Said town of Knox and the Sum of one dollar and four cents for and on Account of the other part therof. lying and being in the Said town of New Scotland, That of the Said children so as above Stated to have been taught in our Said district, the number belonging to that part of Said district lying in the -

[next page]

-Said town of Knox is forty one and that the number belonging to the other part thereof, lying in the Said town of New Scotland is four, That of the Said Children. between the Said ages of five and Sixteen years so as above Stated to reside in our District the number residing in that part of the Said district lying in the said town of Knox is fifty two and that the number residing in the other part thereof lying in the said town of New Scotland is four- And we further report, that our School has not been visited by any of the inspectors of Common Schools during the Year preceding this report, and the sum paid for teachers wages over and above the public moneys apportioned to said district. during the Same Year Amounts to Fifty dollars and twenty cents of which Sum Forty five dollars and fifty four cents were paid by that part of the district lying in the town of Knox and four dollars and Sixty Six cents by the part lying in the town of New Scotland,- Dated at Knox this first day of January in the Year of our Lord one thousand eight hundred and thirty nine, - - - -

Derrick Van. Schaack \
John B. Winne } trustees
John Mc Williams /

[1839 February]

At a Special meeting of the freeholders and inhabitants of School District No.5 in the town of Knox convened at the School house in Said district on the 9th Feb. 1839 by order of the trustees of Said dist. and agreeable to legal notice given by the clerk of Said district for the purpose of Electing a libarian in Said district and for the transaction of Such other business as the meeting may deem proper. --

1st. Resolved by said meeting that Jacob P. Mesick be the librarian of said district.

2nd. Resolved that no book Shall be drawn from the District library by any of the inhabitants thereof for a longer time than one month before the same Shall be returned, and every person neglecting or refusing to return the book or books as above Specifyed Shall be liable to a penalty of twelve & a half cents for every month after the first month and in that proportion for any period of time, and all damages done to the book or books to be appraised by the librarian paid

3rd. Resolved by Said meeting that the penaltyes [sic] & damages above Specified must all be paid by the person or persons lyable [sic] therefore before they shall be intitled [sic] to draw any other book or books from Said library. all payments to be made to the librarian of said district. –

[next page]

-4th. Resolved by Said meeting that two thirds of the public money be paid for the winter School & one third for the Summer School or other parts of the Year as the trustees of Said district may deem proper,-

Dated at School District No.5 in the town of Knox this 9th day of February 1839, -

Derrick Van Schaack Chairman

J. P. Mesick Dist. Clerk

[1839 April]

John B. Winne, one of the trustees of School District No.5 in the town of Knox, Received the public money from the Commissioners of Common Schools of Said town the amount of which was thirty Six dollars and thirty cents teachers money and nine dollars and Seven cents library money

Knox April 30th 1839 (teachers money $ 36..30

J.P. Mesick Dist. Clerk (library money.. 9.. .7
$ 45..37

Received from John B. Winne one of the trustes of School district No.5 in the town of Knox - nine dollars and Seven cents as library money for said district.) J.P. Mesick librarian

Knox April 30th 1839,

John Mc Williams one of the trustes of School district No.5 in the towns of Knox & New Scotland Recd. Publick money from the Commissioners of Common Schools of the town of New Scotland the Amount of which was $3..38 three dollars thirty eight cents

whole Amount of teachers - (teachers money $2..71
money $ 39. 01 (library money- 0..67
library - 9..74 (total Amount - $3..38
Total - 48..75

library money paid to J Hungerford $9..74 1840. May [This line was written by the same writer, but with a different pen.]

[1839 October]

At an annual meeting of the freeholders an inhabitants of School district number five in the town of Knox & New Scotland held pursuant to adjournment at the School house in Said District on the 26th day of October 1839. Derrick Van Schaack was chosen Moderator and Jacob P. Mesick was present as District Clerk,- Resolved unanimously that Isaac Hungerford. Storm Flansburgh and John Mc Williams be the trustees for the insuing year and Jacob P. Mesick Clerk and Jacob Brunk collector for the the [sic] insuing Year & Jacob P. Mesick librarian for the insuing year

Resolved that there be a tax of ten Dollars levyed on the district for the purpose of repairing the School house in Said district Resolved that the next annual meeting be on the last Saturday in October next at three oclock P.M. by adjournment Said meeting to be at the School house in Said district Dated at School District No.5 in the town of Knox this 26th day of October A.D. 1839

Derrick Van Schaack
Jacob P. Mesick Clerk

[1840 January]

To the Commissioners of Common Schools of the town of Knox,- We the trustees of School district No.5 formed partly out of the Said town of Knox and partly out of the adjoining town of New. Scotland. do in conformity with the Statute for the Support of Common Schools.-

Certify and report: That the whole time any School has been kept in our district during the year ending on the date hereof and Since the date of the last report for Said district is Seven months and that the time during Said year & Since the date of the Said last report Such School has been kept by teachers after obtaining a certificate of qualification from the inspectors of common Schools is Seven months- That the amount of money received in our district from the Commissioners of common Schools during the Said year & Since the date of the Said last report excepting library money is $39..01 and that the Said Sum has been applyed to the payment of the compensation of teachers employed in Said district & qualified as the Statute prescribes,- That the Amount of library money received in our district from the Comissioners of common Schools during Said year & Since the date of Said last report is $9..74 and that the Said Sum has been applied to the purchase of a library for the district That the number of volumes belonging to the district –

[next page]

-library and on hand is 46, That the number of children taught in Said district during Said year & Since Said last report is 43.- And that the number of children residing in our district on the last day of december last who are over five and under Sixteen years of age is 50,- and that the names of the parents or other persons with whom Such children respectively reside & the number residing with Each are as follows Viz:-

Isaac Hungerford 6. Aaron C. Hellenbeck 5. Jacob P. Mesick 4. John Reamer 4. Casper Decker 4. John Mc Williams 4. Wilhelmas Pier 3. Derrick Van Schaack 3. William Tygert Jr 3. Jacob Brunk 3. Francis Hurst 2. John B. Winne 2. Andrew Secor 2nd 2. Henry Cornelius 1. Storm Flansburgh 1. William Secor 1. Wm. Dennis 1. Leonard Schermerhorn 1.- And we do further Specify and report that of the Said Sum of money So as above Stated to have been received in our Said district to be applied to the payment of teachers wages the Sum of $36..30.cts was received for and on Account of that part of Said district lying in the Said town of Knox and the Sum of $2..71 cts was received for & on Account of the other part thereof lying and being in Said town of New-Scotland- That of the Said Sum of money

So as above Stated to have been received in our dis-district [sic; the first "dis" is at the end of a line.] for the purchase of a district library the Sum of $9..07 was received for & on Account of that part of Said

continued third page following - - - -

[three pages later]

=district lying in Said town of Knox and the Sum of $00..67 cents for and on account of the other part thereof lying in the Said town of New Scotland - That of the Said children so as above Stated to have been taught in our district the number belonging to that part of Said district lying in Said town of Knox is 40, And that the number belonging to the other part thereof lying in Said town of New Scotland is 3. That of the Said children between the ages of five & Sixteen years so as above Stated to reside in our district, the number residing in that part of Said district in Said town of Knox is 46. And that the number residing in the other part thereof lying in Said town of New Scotland is 4. - And we further report that our School has not been visited by the inspector of Common Schools or any one of them during the year preceeding [sic] this report – and the Sum paid for teachers wages over and above the public moneys apportioned to Said district during the Same Year amounts to $25..03. of which Sum $23..90 were paid by that part of Said district lying in the town of Knox and $1..13 by that part lying in the town of New Scotland, Dated at Knox this first day of January in the year of our Lord one thousand Eight hundred and forty - Isaac Hungerford }

(A Copy) John McWilliams } trustees

[1840 February & March]

[The following table was written near the back of the book and is spread across two pages. There were two more columns: "condition good" and "condition bad"; all books were in "Good" condition.]

Time of delivery 1840	Title and No. of book	To whom	When returned
Feb 3rd	Life of Wayne & Vane 73	I. Hungerford	17th Feb
Feb 8th	Life of Smith & E.Allen 70	S. Flansburgh	21 Feb

Feb 13th	power of religion No 61	J.B. Winne	24th Feb
Feb 17th	Spectator 1st Vol 84	B. Secor	1st Mar
Feb 17th	polar Seas & Regions 67	P. Pangburn	29th Feb
Feb 19th	Natural History birds 82	J. Reamer	29th Feb
Feb 21	a natural philosophy 83	S. Flansburgh	5th Mar
Feb 24th	Dwights lives of the signers91	John B. Winne	9th Mar
Feb 24th	Franklins life 1st Vol. 51	A. Vanschaack	2nd Mar
~~Feb 24th~~	~~Franklins life 2nd Vol.~~	- - - -	- - - -
Feb 24th	Stark Brown & Allen 70	D. VanSchaack	1st Mar
Feb 29th	Benadick Arnold 72	John Reamer	13th Mar
March 1st	Gouldsmiths History of Green81	K. Vanschaack	15th Mar
March 2nd	natural history Quadrupeds 89	J. McWilliams	17th Mar
March 2nd	Franklin 2nd Vol. 52	A. Vanschaack	14th Mar
March 3rd	Stark Brown MontAllen 70	I. Hungerford	17th Mar
March 5th	Wilson & Smith 71	S. Flansburgh	19th Mar
March 9th	lives of the Signers 91	Wm Tygert fam	27th Mar
March 15th	Franklin's 2nd Vol. 52	R. Reamer	22nd Mar
March 15th	Armstrong gardening 88	D. Vanschaack	29th Mar
March 15th	Phips Putman & 76	D. VanSchaack	29th Mar
March 19th	Putman [Warrers?] & 79	S. Flansburgh	3rd Apr

[In the "When returned" column, the dates were abbreviated in the transcription to fit the column; in the original, with the exception of Feb 21, 24, 29, & 29, the dates in this column were spelled-out.]

[1840 March thru June]

[The following table was written near the back of the book and is spread across two pages. There was one more column – "Condition." All books were in "Good" condition.]

1840 Time of Delivery	Title and No. of Book	To Whom	When returned
22nd March	History of Rome No 87	R. Reamer	5th April
22nd March	Wilson & Smith 71	I. Hungerford	6th April
25th March	Spectator 1st Vol - 84	P. Pangburn	8th April
29th March	Spetator [sic] 2nd Vol - 85	D. VanSchaack	12th April
29th March	power of Religion - 96	K. Van Schaack	12th April
3rd April	W.Phips putman Davidson & 76	S. Flansburgh	17th April
12th April	Spectator 1st Vol 84	K. Van Schaack	27th April
12th April	Spectator 2nd Vol - 85	D. Van Schaack	27th April
12th April	Humboldts Travels 80	R. Reamer	26th April
17th April	Pinkney Ellery Mather 75	S. Flansburgh	3rd May
27th April	Spectator 1st Vol 84	Eve. Van Schaack	9th May
27th April	History of birds - 82	D. Van Schaack	9th May
3rd May	Edwards & Brainard 77	S. Flansburgh	17th May
3rd May	Power of religion 96	I. Hungerford	25th May
9th May	Stark Brown Montgomery allen 70	J.McWilliams Junr	24th May

9th May	Franklin's life & works - 51	K. Van Schaack	23rd May
9th May	Pursuit of Knowledge 1 Vol – 55	D. Van Schaack	23rd May
9th May	Plutarck lives Vol 1st 92	R. Reamer	23rd May
17th May	Polar Seas & regions 67	S. Flansburgh	2nd June
23rd May	pursuit of knowledge 2 Vol 56	D. Van Schaack	7th June
23rd May	Life of John Eliot by G.Francis 74	D. Van Schaack	7th June
2nd June	Power of Religion 96	John Reamer	22nd June

[1840 October]

1840. October 24th Notice,s for an Annual Meeting to be held on the 31st instant at the School house at 3. P.M. posted up in four of the most public places in the District by me Jacob P. Mesick District Clerk,

[1840 October]

At an annual Meeting of the freeholders and inhabitants of School District Number five in the towns of Knox and New Scotland held pursuant to adjournment at the School house in Said district on the thirty first day of October 1840. – Storm Flansburgh was Chosen Chairman and Jacob P. Mesick was present as district Clerk. – Resolved that Jacob Brunk Henry Warner Jun. and John McWilliams be the trustees for the insuing Year and Jacob P. Mesick District Clerk and Albert Van Schaack Collector. Resolved that Isaac Hungerford be the librarian for the insuing Year. Resolved unanimously that there [be] a tax of ten dollars levyed on Said district for the purpose of repairing the school house in said district Resolved that the next annual Meeting be on the last Saturday in October next at three Oclock P.M. at the School house in Said district by adjournment. –

Dated at School district Number five in the town of Knox this 31st day of October 1840

Storm Flansburgh Charm.}
Jacob P. Mesick Clk. }

[The following was written on a page at the back of the book.]

1840 April School money $ 32 85
8 20 library money
41..05
3 40 [in pencil]
32..85 [in ink] $ 44 .45 [in pencil] 8 20 [in ink]
68
8 . 88

1841 April Knox Public money $35..22 [in ink]
Library money- 9..50
total $44,.72
1842

[The remainder of the page is in pencil and apparently is part of the 1840 calculation.]

New Scotland -3 40
68 library money
2 .72 teachers money
whole amount $3 .40

Swan 4
McWilliams 5
9 New Scotland

32 85
2 72
35 .57

[The following was written at the back of the book, on a page just before the calculations above.]

1841 April Jacob Brunk one of the trustees of School Dist. No. 5 formed partly of out of the town of Knox and partly out of the town of New Scotland Received public money from the Commissioners of Knox the Amount of which was $44..72 of which Sum $35.22 was teachers money the library money was - 9..50 [The "9..50" was aligned under the "$35.22".]

1841 April John McWilliams one of the trustees aforesaid Received Public money from the Commissioner of New Scotland aforesaid the

amount of which was $4..19 of which Sum --- $3.36 was teachers money, and the library was - - 0..83} paid C. Farley teacher $22..22 paid Jemima Van Schaack for teaching - - - 13..00 [The underlined numbers were aligned and the two teachers' wages were aligned.]
the above payments made by Jacob Brunk trustee in 1841

[1841 October]

At an Annual meeting of the freeholders and inhabitants of School District Number five in the town of Knox and New Scotland held pursuant to adjournment at the School house in Said district on the thirtieth day of October A.D. 1841. Derrick Van Schaack was Chosen Chairman and Jacob P. Mesick was present as District Clerk. – Resolved by Said meeting that Andrew Secor 2nd John Reamer and John McWilliams be the trustees for the insuing year and Jacob P. Mesick District Clerk. Derrick Van Schaack librarian and Storm Flansburgh Collector for the insuing year Resolved that the library money hereafter Received by [sic] applied to the payment of teachers wages if allowed by law Resolved that Isaac Hungerford & Jacob P. Mesick Select the Books for the library for the present year Resolved that the next annual meeting be on the last Saturday in October next at Six Oclock P.M. at the School house in Said District by adjournment

Dated at School District {Derrick Van Schaack Charm.
No. 5 this 30th Oct A.D. 1841 {Jacob P. Mesick Dist. Clk.

[1842 October]

At an annual meeting of the freeholders and inhabitants of School District Number five formed partly out of the town of Knox and partly out of the adjoining town of New Scotland in the County of Albany. held pursuant to adjournment at the School house in Said district on the 29th day of October instant. Isaac Hungerford was Chosen Chairman and Jacob P. Mesick was present being the Clerk of Said district, Resolved by Said meeting that Isaac Hungerford Storm Flansburgh and John McWilliams be the trustees for the insuing year and Jacob P. Mesick Clerk of Said district for the insuing year and John B. Winne librarian and Albert Van Schaack Collector,

Resolved by Said meeting that all the library money Recd. by Said district for the insuing year be paid to the teacher or teachers in Said district,

Resolved that the next annual meeting in Said district be on the first Saturday of november next at Six Oclock P.M. at the School house in Said Dist. by adjournment.

Dated at School district } Isaac Hungerford Chair.
No. 5 this 29th Oct. A.D. 1842} Jacob P. Mesick Dist. Clk.

[The following receipt was written on the last page of the book.]
1843 April 4th School District No. 5
Received from the Commissioners of Common School public money for said district $29..60 teachers money
& library money – 7..40
whole amount - $37..00 [The figures were aligned.]

[1843 November]

At an annual meting [sic] of the freeholders and inhabitants of school District number five formed partly out of the town of Knox and partly out of the adjoining town of New Scotland in the county of Albany held persuant to adjournment at the school house in district number five on the 5th day of November instant John McWilliams was chosen Chairman and Albert Van Schaack was preasant as being the cleark. Resolved by said meeting that John McWilliams was chosen trustee for one year William Secor was chosen trustee for two years and William Hungerford was chosen trustee for three years Albert Van Schaack was chosen Clerk for the ensuing year and John B Winney librarian and John L. Winney Collector Resolved by said meeting that all the library money Received by said district for the ensuing year be paid to the teacher or trustees in said district

Resolved that the next annual meeting in said district be on the first Saturday of november next at Six oclock PM at the school house in said district by adjournment

Dated at School District } John McWilliams chair
No. 5 this 5th Nov AD 1843 } Albert Van Schaack Dist Clerk

[1844 January]

Of Trustees of School District where the District is formed out of two or more ajoining towns to the Town Superintendant of Common School of each town from which said District is in part composed - -

To the Town Superintendant of Common Schools of the Town of Knox - -

We the trustees of school district number five formed partly out of said town and partly out of the ajoining town of New Scotland do

Of Trustees of School District where the Distri
is formed out of two or more ajoining towns
to the Town Superintendent of Common School
of each town from which said District is
in part composed — —
To the Town Superintendent of Common School
of the Town of Knox — —
We the trustees of school district number
five formed partly out of said town and
partly out of the ajoining town of New
Scotland do in conformity with the statute
relating to Common School certify and report
That the school house in said district is
situated in the town of Knox — —
That the whole time any school has been
kept in our district during the year ending
on the date hereof and since the date of the
last report for said district is Ten months
and that the time during said year and since
the date of said last last report such
school has been kept by Teachers after
obtaining a certificate of qulification
according to law is Ten months —

in conformity with the statute relating to Common School certify and report That the school house in said district is situated in the town of Knox - -

That the whole time any school has been kept in our district during the year ending on the date hereof and since the date of the last report for said district is Ten months and that the time during said year and since the date of said last last [sic] report such school has been kept by Teachers after obtaining a certificate of qulification according to law is Ten months - -

[next page]

That no school has been taught in said district by a teacher not so qualified for a longer period than one month That the amount of money apportioned to our district by the Town Superintendent of Common Schools during the said year and since the date of the said last report excepting library money is Thirty one dollars and eighty five cents and that [the?] said sum has been applied on our order to the payment of the compensation of teachers employed is [sic] said district and licensed as the Statues prescribed. That the amount of library money received in our district from the Town Superintendant of Common Schools during said year and since the date of said last report is Seven dollars and ninity Six centes and that the said sum has been applied to the purchase of three volumes of the revised Statues That the number of volums belonging to the district library and on hand on the last day of December last is Seventy One That the number of children taught in said district

[next page]

during said year and since said last report is Six two That of the said children seven attended less than two months Thirteen two months and less than four Twenty five four months and less than Six Ten six months and less than eight Seven eight months and less than ten ten months and less than twelve months. [Apparently there were no children in the last category.] And that the number of children residing in our district on the last day of December last who are over five and under sixteen years of age is forty four and the names of the parents or other persons with whom such children respectfuly reside and the number residing with each are as follows

Names of parents	Numb of children	Names of parents	
John McWilliams	3	Isaac Hungerford	6
Storm Flansburgh	1	Jacob Brunk	3
Derrick Van Schaack	3	William Dennis	2
Henry Warner	3	Caper [sic] Decker	4
Margaret Pier	5	John B Winney	2
William Secor	1	John Remer	2
David Schermerhorn	1	Jacob P. Mesic	3
Andrew Secor	1	Henry Cornelius	1

[next page]

And we do further secify [sic] [certify] and report that of the said sum of money so as above stated to have been apportioned to our said district to be applied to the payment of teachers wages the sum of twenty nine dollars and sixty cents was apportioned for and on account of that part of said district lying in said town of Knox and the sum of Two dollars and twenty five cents for and on account of the other part therof lying and being in said town of New Scotland that of the said sum of money so as above stated to have been received in our district for the purchase of a district library the sum of seven dollars and forty cents was received for and on account of that part said district lying in said town of Knox and the sum of fifty six cents for and on account of the other part therof lying and being in the said town of New Scotland That of the said children so as above stated to have been taught in our said district the number belonging to the part of said district lying in said town of Knox is fifty seven and that

[next page]

the number belonging to the other part therof lying in said town of New Scotland is five That of the said children between the said ages of five and sixteen years so as above stated to reside in our district the number residing in that part of said district lying is said town of Knox is forty one and that the number residing in the other part therof lying in said town of New Scotland is three, And we do further report that our school has been inspected by the County Superintendent during the past year once by the Town Superintendent in company with the County superintendent and by said town superintendent separately three times That the sum paid for teachers wages in said district over and above the public moneys apportioned to said district during the same year amounts to thirty four dollars and fifty cents of which thirty two dollars ninety cents were paid by that part of the district lying in the town of Knox and one dollars and sixty cents by that part lying in the town of New Scotland

[next page]

That the school books in use in said district during the said year are the following viz.

History of the United States Mitchels Geography Dabalas Arithmetic Smiths Grammar Hirkhams Grammar Elementry spelling book Easy Reader English Readers.

That there have been private or select schools not incorporated [tang.?] in said destrict during the said year and that the average number of pupils in attendance therein was [   ]

Dated at Knox this first day of January in the year of our Lord one thousand eight hundred and forty four

John McWilliams }
William Hungerford } Trustees

[1844 March]

[The following receipt was written on the last page of the book.]

Bern March 12th 1844

Received of Albert Van Schaack three dollars and seventy cents for Harriet Phillips

(Ruel Phillips

[1844 November]

At an anual meeting of the freeholders and inhabitants of School District Number five formed partly out of the town of Knox and partly out of the adjoining town of New Scotland in the county of Albany held persuant to adjournment at the school house in district No. 5 on the second day of November instant Derrick Van Schaack was chosen chairman and Albert Van Schaack was chosen clerk Resolved by said meeting that John McWilliams be trustee for one year William Secor be trustee for one year William Hungerford be trustee for two years John Remer was chosen librarian it was Resolved that one half public money be kept for summer school it was Resolved that the library money be expended for maps in school

Resolved that the next annual meeting in said district be on the first saturday of November next at six oclock P,M at the school house in said district by adjourmet

Dated at school District No five this Second day of November A.,D1844

{Derrick Van Schaack chairm
{Albert Van Schaack Dist cler.

[1845 ? November 1]

At and annual meeting of the freeholders and inhabitants of school District Number five formed partly out of the town of Knox and partly out of the adjoining town of New Scotland in the County of

Albany held persuant to adjournment at the school house in district number five on the first day of November instant John McWilliams was chosen chairman and Derrick Van Schaack District Clerk It was resolved by said meeting that John McWilliams be trustee for two years Storm Flansburg be trustee for three years William Hungerford be trustee for one year Casper Decker Collector Jacob Brunk librrian It was resolved that wood be furnished for the school for one year by a [tax?] It was resolved by said meeting that ten dollars be raised for the repairs of the school house It was Resolved by said meeting that the public money be paid for the winter School

[next page]

It was resolved by said meeting that our annual meeting be adjourned untill the first Saturday of October Next

Albert Van Schaack Dist Clerk
John McWilliams Chairman

[1845 November 15]

At a special meeting of the legal voters of school district No 5 formed partly out of the town of Knox and partly out of the adjoining town of New Scotland Called by the trustees of said district and held pursuant to special notice at the schoolhouse on the Fifteenth day of November 1845 John McWilliams was chosen moderator and Derrick Van Schaack was present as district clerk the meting was called for the purpose of providing fuel for said district school

Whereas Isaac hungerford agreed to furnish the wood for one year for nine dollars the same to be sutch [sic] as should

[next page]

be approved of by the teacher and the trustees and the same to be cut and split and fit for use and piled against the school house and further mor to make an estimate of the expence for repairing the schoolhouse John McWilliams for [lime?] [$1:-12 ½ cts.?] John Halenbeck 1 Dollar for plastering William Dennis for laber and bourding Halenbeck $1..75 amounting to $12.87 ½ cts to be raised by tax in the aforesaid district

Derrick Van Schaack Dist Clerk
John McWilliams Chairman

[1846 October]

at an anual meeting of the legal voters of school district No 5 in the town of Knox and partly of the a joining town of New Scotland held persuant to a journment at the Scoolhouse on the 6th day of october 1846 Storm Flamsburgh was chosen moderator and Derrick Van Schack was present as district Clrk Resolved that Isac Hungerford be trustee for three years Resolved that John McWilliams be Clerk for the present year

Resolved that Jacob Brunk be reelected as librarian for the ensuing year

at an anual meeting of the legal voters of School
district No 5 in the town of Knox and partly
of the a joining town of New Scotland held
persuant to a journment at the Scoolhouse
on the 6th day of october 1846 Storm Flams
burgh was chosen moderator and Derrick
van Schack was present as district Clrk
Resolved that Isac Hungerford be trustee for three
years Resolved that John McWilliams be Clerk
for the present year
Resolved that Jacob Brunk be reelected
as librarian for the ensuing year
Resolved that two thirds of the publick moey
be paid for the Winter School and one third for
the sumer School
Resolved that fuel be provideed for the ensuing
year according to the valuation of each inhabitant
Resolved that this meeting adjourn til the first
Saturday of october 1847

Resolvd that two thirds of the publick moey be paid for the Winter School and one third for the Sumer School

Resolved that fuel be provideed for the ensuing year according to the valuation of each inhabitant

Resolved that this meeting adjourn til the first Saterday of october 1847

[1847 October]

At an anual meeting of the legal voters of school district No 5 in the town of Knx and partly of the ajoining town of Newscotland held persuant to ajournment at the school house on the 9th day of October 1847, Derrick Van Schaack was Chosen moderator John McWilliams was present as district Clerk

Resolved that John McWilliams [Jr?] be trustee three years
Resolved that Albert White be Clerk for the ensuing year
Resolved that William Dennis be Collector for the ensuing year
Resolved that John Reame be librarian for the ensuing year

Resolved that this meeting be adjourned till the first Saturday in October AD 1848

the Amount of public money from Knox is $20::52 Cts
the Amount of library money is $5:22 Cts
from New scotland $1,68 Cts library 72 Cts

[1848 October]

at an anual meeting of the legal voters of school district No 5 in the town of Knox and partly of the ajoining town of Newscotland held pursuant to ajournment at the schoolhouse on the 7th Day of October 1848 Isaac Hungerford was chosen moderator John McWilliams Secretary

Resolved that John B [The ink changed from black to blue at this point on this page, but the same person continued writing.] Winney be trustee for three years

Resolved that Derrick Van Schaack be Clerk for the ensuing year
Resolved that William Dennis be Collector for the ensuing year
Resolved that John McWilliams be librarian for the ensuing year

Resolved this meeting be adjourned till the first saturday in October AD 1849

[1849 October]

At an anual meeting of the legal voters of school district No 5 in the town of Knox and partly of the adjoining town of Newscotland held pursuant to ajournment at the schoolhouse on the [6th?] Day of October 1849 John Pitcher was chosen moderator Derrick Van Schaack secretary

Resolved that William Secor be trustee for three years

Resolved that Derrick Van Schaack be Clerk for the ensuing year

Resolved that John Oliver be collector for the ensuing year

Resolved that Adam Reamer be librarian for the ensuing year

Resolved this meeting be adjourned till the first Saturday in October AD 1850

[1850 February]

At a special meeting of District No 5 of the town of Knox called by the trustees of said district and held pursuant to special notice at the School house on the [2nd?] day of February 1850 John McWilliams was chosen chairman and Derrick Van Schaack was present as district Clerk. Resolved that the district pay the teacher $10 per month for three months and John B. Winney $4 per month for board

[1850 October]

At an anual meeting of the legal voters of school district No 5 of the town of Knox and partly of the ajoining town of Newscotland held pursuant to ajournment at the schoolhouse on the 5th day of October 1850

John Oliver was chosen chairman and Derrick Van Schaack was present as District Clerk

Resolved that John McWilliams Jun be trustee for three years and Derrick Van Schaack be Clerk for the ensuing year Isaac Hungerford was chosen librarian for the insuing year

Resolved that John Oliver be Collector for the insuing year Resolved that their shaall be six months schooling the insuing year three months in winter and three in summer One half of the public money to be paid for the winter and the other half for the summer school

fuel to be provided by the District

Resolved this meeting be ajourned till the first saturday in October 1851

[1851 January]

~~At a special meeting of school District No 5 of the town of Knox and partly of the ajoining town of Newscotland~~

At a special meeting of the legal voters Called by order of the trustes of District No 5 of the town of Knox and partly of the ajoining town of Newscotland held at the school house on saturday the 25th of January 1851 Albert Van Schaack was chosen moderator and Isaac Hungerford Clerk pr[o] tem the object of the meeting was to rais a tax for the support of the school for the present year

Resolved that a sum of thirty dollars be raised by tax $30

Albert Van Schaack {Moderator
Isaac Hungerford {Clerk pro tem

[1851 October]

at an anual meeting of the legal voters of school District No 5 of the town of Knox and partly of the ajoining town of Newscotland held pursuant to ajournment at the schoolhouse on the 18th Day of October 1851 John Oliver was chosen chairman and Derrick Van Schaack was present as District Clerk

Resolved that Adam Reamer be trustee for three years and Derrick Van Schaack be Clerk for the ensuing year Isaac Hungerford be librarian fo the insuing year and William Pier be Collector for the insuing year

Resolved that $25 be raised by tax to pay the Teachers wages for the insuing year

Fuel raised by stipulated quantity by each inhabitant

J..MW.	½ Cord	John Oliver	½ Cord
Isaac H	½	Jacob Cornelius	¼
D V S	½	Nicholas R W	½
William Pier	¼	Adam Reamer	½
William Secor	½	Nicholas Livingstone	1/3

Robert Hurst ½ Jacob Pier ¼

the wood to be measured by the teacher

[next page

Resolved that this meeting be adjourned till the first saturday in October, 1852

[1852 April]

At an adjourned meeting of the legal voters of district No 5 in the town of Knox and New Scotland on the 29th Day of April 1852

Resolved that this meeting be adjourned
till the first saturday in October, 1852

At an adjourned meeting of the legal voters of
district No 5 in the town of Knox and New Scotland
on the 29th Day of April 1852
John Oliver was chosen moderator and Derrick Van
Schaack was present as district Clerk
The writen Consent of the town Superentendants of
common schools of the Towns having been read
stating that in their opinion the removal of the site
of the schoolhouse in said district is necessary, and
it having been mooved and seconded that the
present site of the school house in the said district
be Changeed and that a site be selected on the bush
lot of William Secor on the road leading from
Adam Reamers to William Secors on the south side
of said road the site is located 56 Yards from the
fence that bounds the west side of said Lot to the west
Corner of said site and 12.5 yards from the east
corner of said site to a barn on the oposite side
of the road Owned by Andrew Grass be

John Oliver was chosen moderator and Derrick Van Schaack was present as district Clerk

The writen Consent of the town Superentendants of Common schools of the Towns having been read stating that in their opinion the removal of the site of the school house in said district is necessary. and it having been mooved and secondid that the present site of the school house in the said district be Changeed and that a site be selected on the bush lot of William Secor on the road leading from Adam Reamers to William Secors on the south side of said road the site is locatid 56 Yards from the fence that bounds the west side of said Lot to the west Corner of said site and 125 Yards from the east corner of said site to a barn on the opasite side of the road Owned By Andrew Grass be

[next page]

designated as the site of a school house for the said district and the questions taken by ayes and noes it was carried a majority of all those present at sutch adjourned meeting voting for sutch removal an in favor of such new site. Derrick Van Schaack Isaac Hungerford, Storm Flansburg, William Secor William Pier, John Reamer, Albert White, Andrew Grass, Adam Reamer those who votid in the negative John B Winney, Jacob Cornelius, John McWilliams, John McWilliams Ju, this is to take effect on the first day of May

Resolved that the trustees build a school house on said site and the district will bear them out in it

[1852 October 16]

At an anual meeting of the legal voters of school District No 5 of the town of Knox and partly of the adjoining town of Newscotland held pursuant to adjournment at the schoolhouse on the 16th day of October 1852. John McWilliams was chosen moderator and Derrick Van Schaack was present as district Clerk

[next page]

Resolved that William Secor be realectid as trustee and John Oliver be District Clerk and William Pier was realectid Collector and Storm Flansburg was elected librarian

Resolved that the district rais ten dollar for stove pipe and other expences Resolved that Adam Reamer furnish the wood for the district for one year ready for the stove for eight dollars

Resolved that this meeting be adjourned till the first Saturday of October 1853 at 6 Oclock PM

[1852 October 30]

At a Special Meeting of the legal voters of Dist No 5 in the town of Knox and adjoining town of Newscotland held at the school house in pursuance of notice to all the legal voters therein on the 30th day of October 1852 John McWilliams was Chosen Moderator and John Oliver presant as Dist Clerk Resolved that the Sum of two hundred Dollars be voted for bilding the School house and the voters in the Affurmative were John Oliver Storme Flansburg Adam Reamer John McWilliams William Dennis

[next page]

Andrew Grass William Secor those in the Negative where Jacob Pier Robert Hurst

Knox October the 30th 1852 John Oliver Dist Clerk

[1853 April – This page was at the beginning of the book.]

at a special meeting of the legal voters of school district No. 5 formed partly of the town of Knox and partly out of the adjoining town of New scotland called by the trustees of said district and held pursuant to special notice at the school house on the 29th day of April 1853 John M Williams was chosen Chairman and John Oliver was present as district Clerk

Resolved that the fence be made by the [employees?] of said district on Saturday the 30th day of April 1853 Albany [The word "Albany" and a few practice strokes are in a different color ink.]

[1853 October]

At an anual meeting of the legal voters of School district No 5 of the town of Knox and partly of the adjoining town of Newscotland held pursuant to adjournment at the schoolhouse on the 22nd Day of October 1853

Derrick Van Schaack was chosen moderator and John Oliver was present as district Clerk

Resolved that abraham McWilliams be trustee and Storm Flansburg be [Clerk?] and William Denis Be Collector for the ensuing year

Resolved that Adam Reamer be Librarian for the ensuing year

Resolved that the fuel be raised by tax for the ensuing year

Resolve that William Secor furnish the wood for one year for twelve dollars

Resolved that this meeting ajourn till the first saturday of October 1854

[1854 October]

At an anual meeting of the legal voters of the school district N 5 of the town of Knox and partly of the ajoining town of Newscotland held pursuant to adjournment at the scool house on the 7 Day of October 1854 Albert White was chosen moderator and Storm Flansburgh was present as District Clerk Resolved that Robert Hurst and John Oliver bee trustees and Storm Flansburgh be Clerk and Jacob Cornelius be Collector for the ensuin year

Resolved that Adam reamer be libraraan for the ensuin year

Resolved that the fuel be raised by tax for the ensuin year

Resolved that William secor furnish the Wood for one year for twelve dollars

Resolved that this meting ajourn till the first saturday of October – 1855

[1855 ?]

[The following, on the same page as the preceeding, is in a different handwriting.]

At the anuel meting held in School district No 5 William Secor Chosen Charmen John Ketcham district Clerk [footend?]

[next page]

Resolved that David [Bradt?] Jun is electted trustee and Peter Basler district clerk William Denis be Chosen collector for the ensuing year Albert White be librarien for the ensuing year

Resolved the fuel be rased by a tax for the insuing year Resolved that William Secor furnish the Wood for one year for [ ]9 dollars

Resolve that this meting be ajourned until the first saturday of october 1856

[1856 October]

[This page is in pencil.]

Anuel Meting held October the 18 – 1856 [Benjumen?] Secor Was [Caled?] As Charmen Wm Secor Clerk for the Present Meting Resolve that Georg Pilcher be District Clerk for the in Suing year Resolved that Wm Denis be Colecter for the in Suing year

Resolve that Albert White be liberian for the in Suing year

Resolve that the fuel Be raised By tax for the in Suing year

Resolve that Adam Reamer find the Wood for the insuing year for Nine Dollars fifty Six Cents $9-56

Resolved this Meting Be Adgerned til the first Saterday in October 1857

[1857 October]

[Only the first three words are in ink; the rest is in pencil.]

Anual meting held October the 3th 1857 William Secor was chosen chairman

Resolved that Henry Ketcham be trustee for three years, Resolved that George Pitcher be district Clerk for the in suing year, Resolved that Jacob Cornelius be Collector for the in suing year, Resolved that Albert white be librarian for the in suing year,

Resolved that the fuel be rais by tax for the in suing year,

Resolved that Robert Hurst furnish fuel for one years for $9..75 cts

Resolved this meting be rejourn til the first Saturday in October next 1858

[1858 October 12]

[This page is in pencil. The second paragraph is crossed out with two large X's.]

Anuel meeting held October the 12th 1858

~~William Secor was chosen chairman Resolve that Nichaelos Winne, Robert Hurst, David Bradt be trustees For the insuing year~~

Resolved that George Pitcher be District Clerk for the insuing year,

Resolved that Albert White be Collector for the insuing year,

Resolved that Albert White be librarian for the insuing year

Resolved that Robert Hurst Furnish the fuel for one year for eight dollars and eighty seven cents,

Resolved that a tax be rais for 3, Benches, George Pitcher make them

Resolve this meting be redjourn til the next, anuel meting

October ,AD 1859

Resolve that half the public money be use for winter school,

[1858 October 22]

[This page is in pencil.]

Special meeting held October the 22 1858

Resolve that Adam Reamer be Chairman of this meeting,

Resolved that Nichalas J Winney be trustee for three years,

Resolved that William Secor be trustee for two years,

Resolved that John Oliver be trustee [and on the next line] tee for one year,

Resolve that David Bradt find the wood one year for Seven dollars and fifty cents, 7,50cts,

Resolved this meeting be rejourned till 2nd tuesday in October next at 7 Oclock AD 1859,

[1859 October]

[The writer appears to be the same as the previous three penciled pages, but is now using ink.]

Anuel meeting held October the 11, AD 1859

Resolved that William Secor be Chairman of this meeting,

Resolved that there be two trustees for the insuing year,

Resoved that George Pitcher be District Cleark for the insuing year,

Resolved that Albert White be librarian for the insuing year,

Resolved that Albert White be Collector for the insuing year,

Resolved that the fuel be Rais by tax,

~~Resolved that William Pier, furnish the fuel for the~~

Resolved that William Secor furnish the fuel for one year, for \$8,62 ½ cts,

Resolved that this meeting be rejournd till 2nd tuesday in October next at 7, Oclock, AD 1860,

[1860 October]
Anuel meeting held October the 9 AD 1860
Resolved that Andrew grass be chairmen of this meeting
Resolved that there be three trustees for the insuing year
Resolve that George Pitcher be District Cleark for the insuing year
Resolved that Robert hurst be trustee for three years,
Resolved that John Oliver be librarien for the insuing year,
Resolved that Albert white be Collector for the insuing year
Resolved that William Secor furnish
[The ink was becoming light; remainder of this page is in pencil.]
the fuell for the insuing year, ten dollars $10,
Resolved that this meeting be rejurnd till October next, AD 1861 at 7 seven Oclock in the evening

[1861 October]
Anuel meeting held October the. 8 AD. 1861,
Resolved that Adam Reamer be chairman Of this meeting,
Res that George Pitcher be District Cleark for the insuing year,
Resolved that David Brat be trustee for three years,
Resolved that Benjamin G Secor be trustee for one year
Resolved that John Oliver be librarian for the insuing year,
Resolved that Albert white be Collector for the insuing year,
Resolved that half the public be use half for winter Season and half summer
Resolved that the fuel be found by the Cord,

Resolved that this meeting be rejourn till second tuesday in October next AD 1862 at 7. Oclock in the evening

[1862 October]
Anuel meeting held October the 14, AD 1862
Resolved that Andrew Grass be chairman of this meeting
Resolved that George Pitcher be District Cleark for the insuing year
Resolved that William Secor be trustee for three years,
Resolved that John Oliver be librarian for the insuing year,
Resolved that Andrew Grass be Collector for the insuing year,

Resolved that half the public money for winter school and half for summer school, [sic]

Resolved that the trustees furnish the fuel for one year,

Resolved that this meeting be rejourn till second tuesday in October next AD 1863 At 7 Oclock in the after noon

[1863 October]

Anuel meeting held October 13, AD 1863,

Resolve that William Secor be chairman of this meeting

Resolved that George Pitcher be District Cleark for the insuing year,

Resolved that William Pier be trustee for three years

Resolved that John Oliver be librarian for the insuing year

Resolved that Andrew Grass be Collector for the insuing year,

Resolved that half the public money be used for the winter school and the remainder for the summer school,

Resolved that the District furnish the fuel for the School,

Resolved this meeting be rejourn till second tuesday in October next AD 1864, at 7 Oclock in the after noon

Resolved that the wood drawd on the first Saturday in december AD 1863

1864/ ["1864/" is in pencil; the remainder of the page is in ink.]

At the anual meeting held Oct 11th 64

Reesolved that Benjamin Secor be Chairman of this meeting

Reesolved that Peter Hungerford be District Clerk for the ensuing year.

Reesolved that David Bradt be Trustee for three Years.

Reesolved that Jacob Pier be trustee for the Term of Two Years.

Reesolved that John Oliver be Librarian for the ensuing year.

Reesolved that Benjamin Secor be Collector for the ensuing Year.

Reesolved that half of the Public money be appropriated to winter school half to the Summer School

Reesolved that this meeting be adjourned until the second Tuesday in Oct 1865 at 7 Oclock

Peter Hungerford
Secratary

1865/ 1865

[This page is in pencil.]

At the anual meeting held Oct 10th 1865 pursuant to call and in [accordance?] to law Benjamin [G?] Secor be Chairman Peter Hungerford Secretary

Reesolved that Nicholas Winne be Trustee for three Years

and that Isaac H Reamer be District Clerk
also John Oliver be Librarian

that Andrew Cornelius be Collector

Resolved that half of the Public money be used for Winter School half to the Summer School when the meeting adjourned

Benjamin [G?] Secor /Chairman

Peter Hungerford Secretary

[next page]

[This page is in pencil.]

it has ben resolved andnd voted that thoes that don't fetch the wood that thay Shall pay at the rate of $4 a cord

it is motion. and that this meting is adjourned til the 2 tusday of next october 1866 at 7 o clock /

Isaac H Reamer
Sectary

Wm Secor	[2/4?]
David Bradt	½
Nicholas P Wine	½
John Pier	½
John P Oliver	½
Jacob Cornelias	½
Adam Reamer	½
Jacob Pier	½
Benjmin Secor	¼
Henry Ketchman	½
Isaac Hungerford	½

[1866 October]

At the anual meting October 9 1866 Resolved William Secor be Charman of this meting Resolved that Isaac H Reamer Distric Clerk for the ensuing year Resolved that Benjman G Secor be trustee for three years Resolved that John Oliver be Libraian for the ensuing year Resolved that William J Secor be Collector for the ensuing year Resolved that The Distric find the wood for the wood [sic] ensuing year Resolved that Half of the Pulic mony be appropiate to winter Scool half to the Sumer Scool Resolved that this meting be adjournd untill the Second Tusday in October 1867 at 7 O clock

Isaac H Reamer
Sectary

[1867 October]

At an anuel meting October 8 1867 Resolved that John Oliver be charman of this meting Resolved that Jacope A Worner District Clerk for the ensuing year Resolved that Lornce Clickman Trustee for three years Resolved that John Oliver be libraian for the Ensuing year Resolved that Andrew Cornelious be Colector for the Ensuingn year Resolved that the District find the wood for the Ensuing year Resolved that thoes that dont fetch wood for the ensuing year Shall be tax at the rate of $4 per cord [The handwriting changed at this point.]

Resolve that this meeting be Adjurned untill the second Tuseday in October 1968 at 7 Oclock

J. A. Warner
Clerk

[1868 October]

At an anuel meting Oct 13th 1868 Resolved that William Secor be Charman of this meeting Resolved that J.A. Warner be District Clerk for the ensuing year Resolved that William Secor be Trustee for three years Resolved that John Oliver be libaran for the Ensuing year Resolve that Jacob Carnealus be Colector for the Ensuing year Resolved that the District find the wood for the Ensuing year Resolved that those that dont fetch wood for the ensuing year shall be taxt at the rate of $4 per Cord Resolved that this meeting be adjurnd untill the second Tusday in October 1869 at 7 Oclock

J. A. Warner
Clerk

[1869 October]

[This page is in pencil.]

At an anuel meting held Oct 19th 1869

Resolve that Niccklu J Winney be Charman of the meeting

Resolve that William Kitcham be Clerk of scool District No 5 fo the ensuing year Resolved that John Pier be Trutee for 3 ensuing years

Resolve that John Oliver be Libarun for the ensuing year

Resolve that Charles Oliver be Collector

Resolve that the Wood be found as the year before

Resolve that this meeting be journd till second tuesday ~~next~~ in Oct. 1870 at 7 O Clock in the evening

Wood List of 1869

[This page is in pencil and close to the back of the book.]

William Secor	½ Cord
John Oliver	½
Bemgam [sic] Secor	¼
John Hungerford	½
Gilbert Vanzant	½
Jacob A. Warner	½
Ambroes Ketcham	¼
Alonzo Ketcham	½
Adam Reamer	½
Fredrick Hurst	½
John Pier	¼
Jacob Cornealus	¼
Larnce Clickman	¼
N. J. Winey	½
William Secor Ju	½

[1870 October]

[This page is in pencil.]

At an anual meeting of the legal voters of School district No 5 in the town of Knox and partly of the adjoining town of New Scotland, Held pursuant to adjournment at the School house, on the 11th October 1870 [A "6" was overwritten with the "7".] Wm H.. Ketcham was appointed for Clerk for the ensuing year.

Resolved that John Hungerford be trustee for the three ensuing years

Resolved that John Oliver be Librarian for the ensuing year

Resolved that Alonzo Ketcham be Collector for the ensuing year

Resolved that ~~that~~ there be a new Roof placed upon the School house some time this fall

Resolved that this meeting be adjourned until the second tuesday in October 1871 at 7 Oclock P.M

[1871 October]

[This page is in pencil.]

At an anual meeting of the legal voters of School district No. 5 of the town of Knox held pursuant to adjournment at the School house on the 10th day of Oct 1871

John Oliver was appointed chairman

Resolved that W H Ketcham be Clerk for the ensuing year

Resolved that Adam Reamer be Trustee for three ensuing years

Resolved that Benjamin G Secor be Collector for three ensuing years

Resolved that John Oliver be Librarian for the ensuing year

Resolved that the wood be furnished as the year before

Resolved that this meeting be adjourned until the second tuesday in October 1872

[1872 October]

At an anual meeting of the legal voters of School district No 5 of the town of Knox held pursuant to adjournment at the school house on the 8th day of Oct 1872 John Oliver was appointed Chairman

Resolved that Wm H Ketcham be Clerk for the ensuing year

Resolved that Jacob A. Warner be trustee for the ensuing year

Resolved that Andrew Cornelius be Collector for the ensuing year

Resolved that N.J. Winne be Librarian for the ensuing year

Resolved that wood be furnished the same as the year befor

Resolved that this meeting be adjourned until the second tuesday in October 1873

Wm H. Ketcham Dist Clerk

[1873 October]

At an anual meeting of the legal voters of school district No. 5 of the town of Knox held pursuant to adjournment at the school house on the 14th day of October 1873

William Secor was appointed Chairman

Resolved that Wm H Ketcham be Dist Clerk for the ensuing year

Resolved that Frederick Hurst be trustee for the ensuing three years

Resolved that Jacob Cornelius be Collector for the ensuing year

Resolved that Ambrose S Ketcham be Librarian for the ensuing year

Resolved that the wood be furnished the same as as [sic] the previous year and that those who ~~are~~ owe the district wood shall draw wood first and that those who do not furnish wood shall be taxed at the rate of $4 per cord

Resolved that this meeting adjourn until the second tuesday in October 1874 at 7 Oclock P.M.

W. H. Ketcham
Dist Clerk

[1874 October]

At an anual meeting of the legal voters of school dist no. 5 of the town of Knox held pursuant to adjournment at the school house in said district on the 13th day of October 1874 [This was written "1873" and the "4" was then written over the "3".]

Benjamin G. Secor was appointed Chairman

Resolved that Wm H.. Ketcham be dist Clerk for the ensuing year

Resolved that Alonzo Ketcham be trustee for the ensuing three years

Resolved that John Hungerford be Collector for the ensuing year

Resolved that Ambrose Ketcham be Librarian for the ensuing year.

Resolved that this meeting adjourn until the second tuesday in October 1874 at 7 Oclock P.M. ["1874" should be "1875".]

W. H. Ketcham dist Clerk

[1875 October]

At an anual meeting of the legal voters of School district No 5 of the town of Knox held pursuant to adjournment at the school house in said district on the 12th day of October 1875, the following resolutions were passed.

[After the next word, the handwriting and ink color change; the word "Resolved" and the previous lines appear to be written by W.H. Ketcham, the remainder by Isaac Reamer.]

Resolved That Isaac H Reamer be dristric Clerk for the ensuing year

Resolved That John Hungerford be truste for three years

Resolved That John H. Wine be truste for the ensuing year

Resolved that John Piere be Colecter for the ensuing year

Resolved that Ambroes Ketchman be librarnan for the ensuing year

Resolved that Neuton Ketchman valuation be equlized with the vauation of the dristric

Resolved that this meeting adjurn until til 1876 the Second tusday in October 1876

[1876 October]

At an anuel meting of the legal voters of School district No 5 of the town of Knox held pursuant to adjurment at the School house in Said distric on the 10 day of October 1876 The following reslution ware pased

Resolved that Isaac H Reamer be clerk for the ensuing yeare

Resolved that Newton Ketchum be trustee for the next three years

Resolved that John Pier be colecter for the ensuing year

Resolved that Ambroes Ketchum be librarin for the ensuing year

resolved that this meting atjurn until the next Sexond tusday in October 1877 afternoon Seven oclock

December 23the 1876

A Specel meting was caled by order of the trustee of Distric No 5 for the purpoes of taking a vote wether wether the distric is in favor of William Ketchman techn School in Said distric [&?] the vote was taken an caried So seide the charman Morgain Secor was nominated Charman

motion made that we atjurn

Isaac H Reamer
Distric Clerk

[1877 ?]

[Based on the handwriting and ink, this list appears to be by Isaac Reamer in 1876 or 1877.]

		Cord
William Secor	will find	½ Cord
John Oliver	- -	½
Benjamin Secor	-	¼
John Hungerford		½
Robert Hurst		½
David Bradt	- -	½
William Pier	- -	¼
Ed Ketchum		½
George Pitcher		½
Adam Reamer		½
Jacob Pier		¼
J Pier		¼
J Cornelius		¼

["J Cornelius" is at the bottom of the page; the following names are written sideways along the right margin.]

Lawrence Clickman	½ [The "2" is overwritten on a "4" or visa versa.]
N Winney	½
R J Hurst	¼

[The following numbers, in pencil and a different handwriting, were just above the wood list.]

, , , , , , , , 24
96 250
62

December 9the 1877

at an anuel meting held by the legle voters of the School distric No 5 of the town of Knox pursuant to atjurnent at the School house in Sed distric on the nthe day of October 1877 the fowlling reslution was apdopted pased

Resolved that Isaac H Reamer be clerk for the ensuing year

Resolved tha William J Secor be trustee for the next three years

Resolved that Morgain Secor be Collecter for the ensuing year

Resolved that Ambroes Ketchman be libraran for the ensuing year

Resolved that the following series of school books be used in school Dist No 5 in the town of Knox Watsons Independent readers and spellers. Barnes brief History of the United States. Clarks Grammar. Monteiths Geographies

[next page]

1877

Davies Arithmetics Payson Dunton and scribners copy book. Davies new Elementary Algebra[ ] &

Resolved that this meting atjurn until the Second tusday in October 1878

Distric Clerk
Isaac H Reamer
[fancy underline]

Dated October 8the 1878

[This page is in pencil.]

at an anuel meting helde by the legal voters of Distric No 5 of the town of Knox Countey of Albany Co. NY purusuin to atjurment on the nithe day of October 1878 the [following?] reslution was apdodted pased

Resolved Isaac H Reamer be clrke for the Ensuing year

Resolved theat Jacope A [Warner?] be trustee for one year

Resolved that John Hungerford be trustee for three years

Resolved that John Pier be Colecter for the ensuing year

Resolved that Ambroes Ketchum be librarian for the ensuing year rosolved that we rais mony for the next yar wode Reosolved that this meting atjurn untill nex Second tusday in Octobr

Isaac H Reamer be Clerk

[1879 October]

Dateted Knox October 14 1879 at an [Here the ink faded and the writer switched to pencil.] anuel meting helde by the legal voters of Distric No 5 of the Towns of Knox Albany [Co.?] NY pursuente to atjurment on the 14 day of October 1879 the Fowling reslution was was adopet and pased resolved that Jacope A Werner be charman

Resolved that Isaac H Reamer Be Distric Clerke for the Ensuing year

Resolved that Alonzo Ketchem Be trustee for the next three years

Resolved that Morgain Secor be Colecter for the ensuing year

Resolved that Ambroes Ketchem be libraian for the ensung year

Resolved that the trustee farnish the woede for the year rsolved that this meting atjurn until the Second tusday in October 1880

Isaac H Reamer Distric Clerke

[1880 October]

[This page is in pencil.]

Dated Knox October12the 1880 at an anueal meting helde by the legle voters of distric No 5 of the town of Knox Albany Co NY pursuant to atjurnment on the 14 [A "2" was overwritten with a "4" or visa versa.] October 1880 the Fowling reslution was adopet and pased resolved that Benjmin G Secor be charman for this meting

Resolved that Isaac H Reamer be distric Clerke for the ensuing year

Resolved that Jacope A Werner be trustee For the ensuing year to fill vacancey Resolved that William J Secor be trustee for three years Resolved that Ambroes Ketchem be librain for the ensuing year Resolved that Benjmin G Secor be colecter for the ensuing year Resolved that this meting cloes until the Seconed tusday in October 1881

Isaac H Reamer Distric Clerke

[1881 October]

[This page appears to be written with a purple water-soluble pencil.]

Dated Knox October 11the 1881 at an anual meting held by the legle voters of Distric No 5 in the town of Knox Albany, Co, NY pursuent to last atjurnment 12 October 12the 1880 The fowling reslution was adopet an pased resolved that William Ketchum be charman for the ensuing year resolved that Isaac H Reamer be Clerke for the ensuing year resolved that Daniel Pitcher be trustee for one year resolved that Jacope A Werner be trustee for three years Resolved that Ambroes Ketchum be libraian for the ensuing year resolved that John Pier be colecter for the ensuing year Resolved that this meting atjurne untill the next Second [tusday?] in October 1882

Isaac H Reamer Clerke

[1882 October]

[This page appears to be written with a purple water-soluble pencil.]

Dated Knox October 10the 182 [sic] at an anuel meting held by the leagle voters of Distric No 5 in the town of Knox Albay Co NY pursuent to last year atjurment 10 deye of October 1881 the fowling reslution was atdoped and pased resolved that John S Secor be charman resolved that Isaac H Reame [sic] be Clerke for the ensuing year Resolved that John S Secor be trstee for the next three years Resolved that John Pier ber colecter for the ensuing year Resolved that Ambroes Ketchum be librain for the ensuing year thare is a motion that the fence around the Schoolhouse shal be fenced on three Side and thoes that has built a pannel of fence shal reacve for each panel the amounte of ech panel wich Shal

[next page]

[This page appears to be written with a purple water-soluble pencil.]

be exempt at the rate wat it cost to build one panel wich names is Jacope A werner William Secor John Pier Adam Reamer motion that the fence Shal be built bye a taxe william Secor [have?] the jobe to make the fence at the rate of 75 cents a panel and to build a gate at the Same rate that he gets for building a pannel of fence Resolved that this meating atjurn

Isaac H Reamer
Distric Clerk

[1883 ? October]

[The second Tuesday of October was the 10th in 1882 and the 9th in 1883.]

[This page is in pencil.]

Dated Knox October 9the 1882 at anuel meting held by the legal voters of distric No 5 in the town of Knox countey of Albay Sta[te] of New York pursuent to last year[s] atjurment 9 day of October 1882 the fowling reslution was adoped Resolved that John S Secor be charman resolved that Isaac H Reamer be clerk for the ensuing year motion that the trustees be elected by balet the motion was pute and cared motion was made that Morgain Secor and John Pier be teller for the Election of Trustee Jacope A Werner was declard Elected Trustee for the ensuing year John S Secor was Elected trustee for tow [sic] years Ambroes S Ketchum was elected for three years for trustee over

[next page]

[This page is in pencil.]

Resolved that John Pier be colecter for the ensuing year

Resolved that Jacope Pier be libraian for the ensuing year

Resolved that we atjurn until the next anuel meting

Isaac H Reamer

Distric Clerk

1882

October 9

[1884 August]

[This page is in pencil.]

Dated Knox Augist 26the 1884 at an anuel meting held by legle voters of Distric No 5 in the town of Knox county of Albany State of New York a ~~Special~~ anual meting was cald by order of the trustees of Sed distric for such bu[s]iness as the meting may deem nessary Cornelias White was nomated charman ~~for this me~~ and caried Isaac H Reamer was nomnated for clerk for the ensuing year and carid William Secor was nomnated for trustee and caried Charles Zimer was nomated to be collector for the ensuing year and it was caried Jacope Pier was nonated for libraan for the ensuing year and caried motion was that the meting atjurn till the next anuel meting

Dated Augist 26the 1884

Isaac H Reamer

Distric Clerk

[1885 August]

At an anuel meeting of the legal voters of school district No 5 formed partly out of the town of Knox and partly out of the adjoining town of New Scotland held pursuant to adjournment at the school house in said district on the 25th day of August 1885. The following resolutions were passed Resolved that Ambrose S Ketcham be chairman Resolved that William H Ketcham be Dist Clerk for the ensuing year Resolved that Nicholas J. Winne be Trustee for the ensuing three years Resolved that Morgan Secor be Collector for the ensuing year Resolved that John Pier be Librarian for the ensuing year Resolved that the school house be repaired within the next year Resolved that this meeting adjourn until the next anual meeting

Dated August 25th 1885 Wm. H. Ketcham

Dated Knox Augist 26 the 1889
at an anuel meting held by legal
voters of Distric No 5 in the
town of Knox countey of Albany
State of New York a Special annuel
meting was cald by order of the
trustees of sed distric for such
buiness as the meting may deem
nessary Cornelias White was nominated
charman ~~for this me~~ and caried
Isaac H Reamer was nominated
for clerk for the ensuing year and caried
William Secor was nominated for
trustee and caried Charles Zimer was nominated
to be collector for the ensuing year
and it was caried Jacob Pier was
nominated for libraan for the ensuing
year and caried motion was that
the meting atjurn till the
next anuel meting
Dated Augist 26 the 1889
Isaac H Reamer
Distric Clerk

[1886 August]

At an anual meeting of the legal voters of school district No 5 formed partly out [of?] the town of Knox and partly out of the adjoining town of New Scotland held pursuant to adjournment at the school house in said district on the 31st day of August. 1886

The following resolutions were passed

Resolved that William H Secor be chairman

Resolved that William H Ketcham be dist Clerk for the ensuing year, Resolved that Morgan Secor be Trustee for the ensuing three years. Resolved that Henry Smith be collector for the ensuing year

Resolved that John Pier be librarian for the ensuing year Resolved that Resolved that [sic] this meeting adjourn until the next anual meeting

Dated Aug 31st 1886 Wm.. H.. Ketcham

Dist Clerk

[1887 August]

At an anual meeting of the legal voters of School district No 5 formed partly out of the town of Knox. and partly out of the adjoining town of New Scotland held pursuant to adjournment at the school house in said district on the 30th day of August 1887 the following resolutions were passed,

Resolved. That Jacob A Warner be chairman

Resolved that William H Ketcham be clerk for the ensuing year.

Resolved Ambrose S Ketcham. and Charles Zimmer be tellers for the election of Trustee

Resolved That John C Pier was duly elected Trustee for three years

Resolved that Henry Smith was elected Collector for the ensuing year

Resolved That Jacob Pier be librarian for the ensuing year

Resolved That this meeting be adjourned until the last tuesday in August 1888

Dated August 30th 1887 Wm.. H.. Ketcham

Dist Clerk

Resolved that the person who will furnish the wood for the ensuing year for the least money shall have the contract

[blank page]

[1888 August]

At an anual meeting of the legal voters of school district No 5 formed partly out of the town of Knox and partly out of the town of New Scotland held pursuant to adjournment at the school house in said district on the 28th day of August 1888. the following resolutions were passed. Resolved that Nichalos J Winne be chairman

Resolved that Wm H. Ketcham be clerk for the ensuing year.

Resolved that Henry Smith and Jas Armstrong be tellers. The following Named persons voted for Trustee. Wm J Winne, Jas A Gardner, Chas A Piers, Morgan Secor, Jas Armstrong, Wm. H. Ketcham, Henry H Smith. After Counting the ballots A. S Ketcham was declared elected Trustee for the ensuing three years. Henry Smith was elected Chairman [sic] for the ensuing year

Resolved that Wm J. Secor be librarian for the ensuing year Resolved that the person who will furnish the wood, and fit it for the stove for the least money shall have the contract

over

[next page]

The contract to furnish the wood for Ten months school was awarded to Wm.. J.. Secor for the consideration of Fourteen dollars and seventy five cents. ($14.75)

Resolved that this meeting adjourn until the last Tuesday in August 1889. at 7 Oclock P.M. Dated August 28th 1888

Wm.. H.. Ketcham Dist Clerk

[1889 August]

At an anual meeting of the legal voters of of [sic] school district No 5 formed partly of the town of Knox and partly of the town of New Scotland held pursuant to adjournment at the school house in said district on the 6th day of August 1889 the following resolutions were passed.

Resolved that Wm J.. Secor be chairman

Resolved that Wm H. Ketcham be clerk for the ensuing year. Resolved that Wm J Secor be trustee for three years

Resolved that Henry H Smith be collector for the ensuing year.

Resolved that Charles Fairs be librarian for the ensuing year

Resolved that the person who will furnish the wood for the least money shall have the contract. The wood to be fitted for the stove. for the ensuing year

Resolved that Wm J Secor have the contract to furnish the wood for the ensuing year for Eightec [sic] dollars ($18)

Resolved that this meeting be adjourned until the first tuesday in August 1890

Wm H. Ketcham {dist clerk

[1890 August]

At an anual meeting of legal voters of school district No 5 formed partly out of the town of Knox and partly out of the town of New Scotland held pursuant to adjournment. at the school house in said district on the 5th day of August 1890 the following resolutions were passed

Resolved that Wm J Secor be chairman

Resolved that Wm H Ketcham be clrk [sic] for the ensuing year

Resolved that Lawrance Warner & Morgan Secor be tellers
Voters Morgan Secor, Jacob A Warner, A.S. Ketcham, Wm J. Secor Lawrance Warner Chas Fairs Geo Brownell Henry Smith, Wm H Ketcham

Jacob A Warner was elected trustee for three years.

Resolved that Henry Smith be collector for the ensuing year

Resolved that Chas Fairs be Librarian for the ensuing year
Resolved that the person who will furnish good dry wood for the least money shall have the contract. fit it for the stove

The contract to furnish the wood for the ensuing year was awarded to Wm J Secor for the consideration of Fourteen ($14) dollars

Resolved that this meeting adjourn until the first tuesday in August. 1891

dated August 5th 1890 W.H. Ketcham dist clerk

[1890 September]

At a special school meeting held at the school house in district No 5 in the town of Knox on the 24th day of September 1890 the following resolutions were passed

Resolved that the old school house be sealed instead of plastered

Resolved that the district be taxed .50cts on every hundred dollars valuation

It was resolved that the Trustees oversee and manage the repairing of the school house

Resolved that if there should not be money enough to finish the school house by taxing the district .50cts on every hundred dollars valuation the trustees shall have authority to [borrugh?] the money and another year there shall be a tax levied on the district to pay the ballance [sic]

Resolved that this meeting adjourn sign di [sic]

[1891 August]

At the anual meeting of school district No 5 in the town of Knox held at the school house in said district on 4th day of August 1891 the following resolutions were passed

Resolved that Wm J Secor be chairman

Resolved that Wm H Ketcham be clerk for the ensuing year

Resolved that Jas A Gardiner and Geo Brownell be tellers to canvass the tickets.

Resolved that Simon P Winne be trustee for the following three years

Resolved that Jas A Gardiner be collector for the ensuing year. Resolved that Ira Secor be librarian for the ensuing year

Resolved that the person who will furnish the wood fitted for the stove, for the least money for one year shall have the contract.

The contract was awarded to Wm J Secor to furnish the wood for one year for $16.75

Resolved that this meeting adjourn until the first tuesday in August 1892

dated August 4th 1891 W H Ketcham dist Clerk

[1892 August]

At an anual meeting of the legal voters of school district No 5 formed partly of the town of Knox and partly of the town of New Scotland, held pursuant to adjournment. at the school house in said district on the 2nd day of August 1892. The following resolutions were passed, Resolved that Jacob. A. Warner be chairman Resolved that William H. Ketcham be clerk for the ensuing year. Resolved that that [sic] Wm J. Secor be trustee for three years by a unanimous vote

Resolved that Henry Smithe be collector the ensuing year Resolved that James Armstrong be librarian for the ensuing year Resolved the person who will furnish the wood for the least money shall have the contract Resolved that the wood shall be dry hard maple wood. The contract to furnish good hard maple wood for one year for School dist No 5. was awarded to Wm J Secor for $14.50 There was a resolution at a special meeting to repair the old school house which has been rescinded and it was resolved by a unanimous vote that the old school house be sold to the higst [sic] bidder. and a new school house built

[1892 September]

At a special meeting held at the school house in school district No 5 in the town of Knox on the 6th of Sept. 1892 the following resolutions were passed

James Armstrong was elected chairman

It was resolved that the school house be painted

It was resolved that the ceiling be shallacked inside and then covered. and finished with hard oil. the casings to be painted. and varnished and doors stained. and varnished

Lawrence. L. Clickman was appointed as a committe to choose a color to paint the outside of the school house.

There was a resolution. and it was passed that the outside be painted two coats, outside

[blank page]

[1893 August]

At an anual meeting of legal voters of school district No 5 formed partly out of the town of Knox and partly out of the town of New Scotland held pursuant to adjournment at the school house in said district on the 22nd day of August 1893 the following resolutions were passed

Resolved that Charles Fairs be chairman

Resolved that Wm.. H.. Ketcham be clerk

James Armstrong was duly elected Trustee for three years

Lawrence Warner Was duly elected collector for the ensuing year. Resolved that Charles Fairs be librarian for the ensuing year

It was resolved and carried that a bill of $28.88/100 dollars against the district be allowed and paid. It was resolved and carried that Fifty dollars be raised by tax for school purposes to be raised in 1893

The contract to furnish the the [sic] wood fitted for the stove was awarded to Eli Secor for the consideration of Fifteen dollars. The wood to be furnished for one year The meeting was adjourned until the next anual meeting

dated August 22nd 1893 W H Ketcham dist clerk

[1894 August]

At an anual meeting of the legal voters of school district No 5 formed partly of the towns of Knox and New Scotland held pursuant to [sic] at the school house in said district on the 7th day of August 1894. the following resolutions were passed. Resolved that Wm J Secor be chairman. Resolved that Lawrence Warner and Peter Devoe. be inspectors. of election.

Wm H Ketcham was elected clerk for the ensuing year Wm J Secor 1 James Armstrong 2 W. McCulloch 3 A.S. Ketcham 4 Jacob A Warner 5 Peter Devoe 6

The above 6 all voted for Wm H Ketcham for clerk

A.S. Ketcham was elected trustee by the following vote. Wm J Secor 1 Jacob A Warner 2. Peter Devoe 3 Lawrence Warner 4 James Armstrong 5

L Warner was a candidate for collector

Ira Secor was elected collector for the ensuing year by the following vote A.S. Ketcham 1 D. McCulloch 2 J A. Warner 3. Peter Devoe 4 Ira Secor 5 Eli Secor 6 James Armstrong 7 Wm. J. Secor 8 Lawrence Warner 9

Ira Secor was elected collector by one majority

Laurence Warner was elected Librarian for the ensuing year by the following vote Dudley McCulloch ["Dudley McCulloch" is the only name here.]

Resolved that $25 dollars be raised toward painting School house. Resolved the $50 dollars be raised for School purposes

[next page]

It was resolved the contract to furnish wood for the ensuing year be let to the lowest bidder.

The contract to furnish wood. fitted for the stove for the ensuing year was awarded to Wm. J. Secor for sixteen dollars

The meeting was adjourned Sine die Wm. H. Ketcham} dist clerk

[1895 March]

[This page is in pencil.]

At a special meeting held at the school house in school district No 5 in the town of Knox formed partly out of the town of Knox and New Scotland the following resolution was passed.

If the trustees do their utmost to hire a teacher and fail therein, and thereby lose the public money to the district they do not thereby become per[s]onally responsible to the district for the money so lost The meeting held March tuesday March 19th 1895

There was a motion made and carried to adjourn sign dei [sic]

W H. Ketcham clerk

[1895 August]

At an anual meeting of the legal voters of School district No 5 formed partly of the town of Knox and New Scotland held pursuant to adjournment at the school house in said district on the 20th day of August 1895 the following resolutions were passed

Resolved that A.S. Ketcham be chairman

" that Wm. J. Secor and Jas Armstrong be talismen that Wm H Ketcham be clerk

Jacob A Warner and Jas Armstrong vote for clerk no opposition

Resolved The following voted for trustee John Hallenbeck John Pier. John Jones Simon P Winne Cyrus Rider Peter Devoe Morgan Secor Wm Devlin. Elmer Griffin Jacob A Warner Ralph Stalker Thomas Cabin Ira Secor A.S. Ketcham Eli Secor Lawrence Warner Wm Jay Secor, Jas Armstrong Wm H. Ketcham

Wm J. Secor Received ten votes. Ralph Stalker received Nine votes Wm J. Secor was was [sic] elected by one Majority

[next page]

The following voted for Collector

John Hallenbeck. Cyrus Ryter Jacob A. Warner John Pier Simon P. Winne Wm Devlin Thomas Cabin Elmer Griffin Ralph Stalker Morgan Secor Peter Devoe John Jones Lawrence Warner Ira Secor A S Ketcham Eli Secor Jas Armstrong Wm. J. Secor Wm H. Ketcham

John Pier received Twelve votes for collector

Morgan Secor Received seven " "

John Pier was elected by five majority

The following voted for Librarian

Jacob A Warner. Wm J. Secor

Lawrence Warner was elected Librarian receiving two votes. no opposition

It was resolved that the person will fornish [sic] the wood for fitted for the stove good Suitable wood for one year Shall have the contract

Ira Secor was awarded the contract to furnish the wood for one year for Ten dollars

It was resolved that Fifty dollars be raised by tax for teachers wages It was resolved that the meeting adjourn Sign die [sic]

Wm H. Ketcham dist Clerk

[blank page, other than a rectangle drawn in pencil and divided into nine rectangles or squares]

[1896 August]

At the anual meeting held at the school house in school district No 5 in the town of Knox on the 4th day of August 1896 the following resolutions were passed

Resolved that A.S. Ketcham be chairman

Lawrence Warner was elected trustee

Resolved that Wm H. Ketcham be clerk ~~that~~ for the ensuing year

Resolved that John C. Pier be collector for the ensuing year

Resolved that the person who will furnish the wood for one year for the least money Shall have the contract

The contract to furnish the wood for one year was awarded to Wm J. Secor for $12 twelve dollars Resolved that fifty dollars be raised by tax on property for teachers wages for the ensuing year

Resolved that this meeting adjourn sign die [sic]

Wm. H. Ketcham
dist clerk

[1897 August]

At the anual school meeting held at the school house in school district No 5 in the town of Knox on the 3d day of August 1897 the following resolutions were passed

Resolved that Wm. J. Secor be chairman

A.S. Ketcham was elected Trustee. There were seven ballots cast for trustee. All for A.S. Ketcham

There was [sic] six ballots cast for district clerk

William H Ketcham received all of them and was elected clerk

Resolved that Ira secor be collector. he was elected by four majority

Resolved that Morgan Secor be librarian the ensuing year

The contract to furnish the wood for one year for the school fitted for the stove was awarded to Wm. J. Secor for Twelve dollars

Resolved that Sixty dollars be raised by tax on property for teachers wages

Resolved that that [sic] this meeting adjourn Sign die [sic]

Wm H. Ketcham dist clerk

[1898 ?]

It has been resolved that the New School house be built on the old site with the exception of additional grounds which Wm. J. Secor has agreed to give. and it was resolved that the new school house be built with its front to the road Resolved that the old school house be sold by the chairman of this meeting to night, The old shool house was sold to Wm J Secor for ($30.) dollars This meeting has adjourned until the first tuesday in August. 1898

Wm H. Ketcham dist clerk

[1899 August]

At an anual meeting of the legal voters of school district No 5 in the town of Knox and New Scotland held at the school house in said district on the first day of August 1899 the following resolutions were passed

Resolved that Wm. J. Secor be chairman

Resolved that Wm H Ketcham and Lawrence Warner inspectors of election

Resolved that Wm..H.. Ketcham be clerk for the ensuing year

Resolved that Dewitt C. Winne be collector for the ensuing year he received a unanimous vote

Resolved that Frank Pitcher be Librarian for the ensuing year. He received a unanimous vote

William J Secor was awarded the contract to furnish the wood fitted for the stove for the ensuing year for $9.50/100 Resolved that $150 be raised for School purposes. It was carried by a unanimous vote

Resolved that his meeting adjourn until the next anual meeting

Wm H. Ketcham} dist clerk

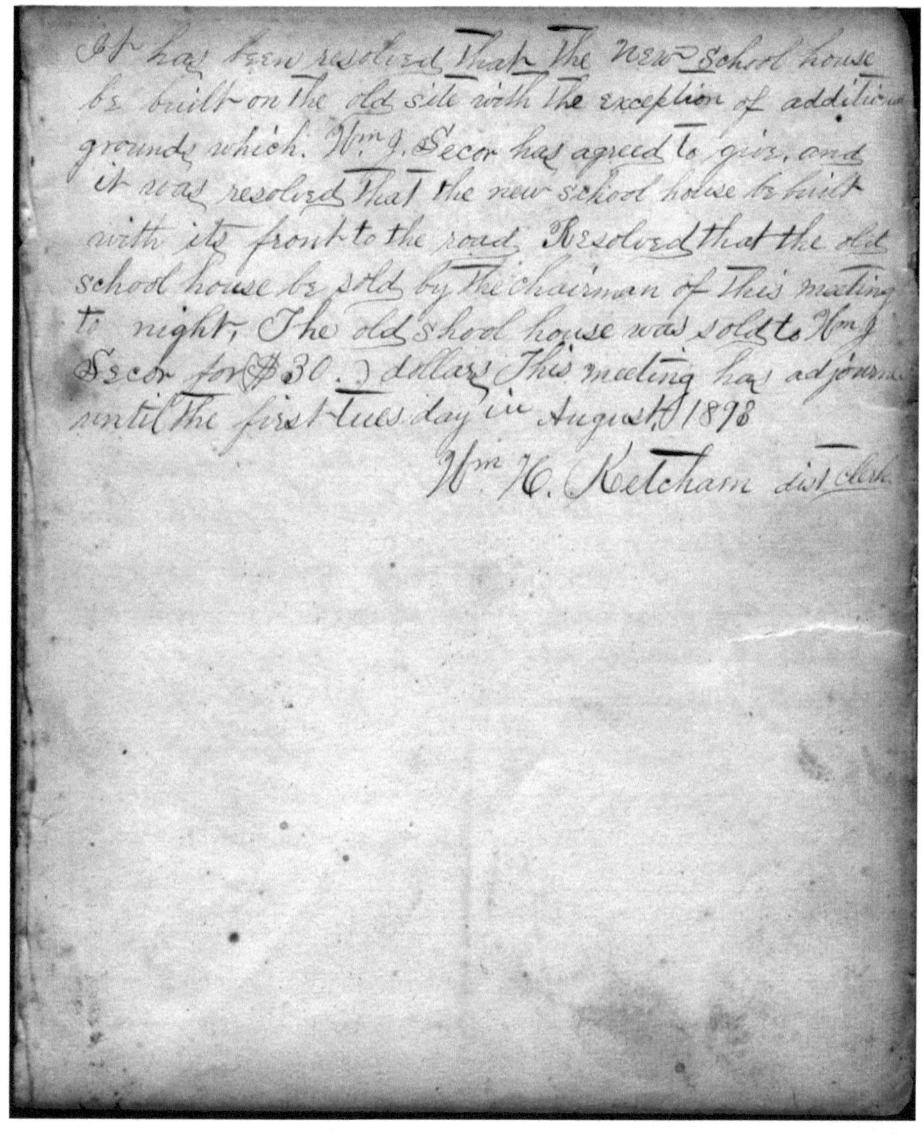
It has been resolved that the new school house
be built on the old site with the exception of additional
grounds which Wm J. Secor has agreed to give, and
it was resolved that the new school house be built
with its front to the road, Resolved that the old
school house be sold by the chairman of this meeting
to night, The old school house was sold to Wm J
Secor for $30.) dollars This meeting has adjourned
until the first tues day in August 1898
Wm H. Ketcham dist clerk

[blank page]

[1900 August]

At an anual meeting of school district No 5 in the town of Knox. and the adjoining town of New Scotland Wm J Secor was elected Chairman

The meeting was held at the school house on the 7th day of August 1900

The following resolutions were passed

Wm H Ketcham was elected clerk

The following voted for Trustee Peter Devoe John Snyder Frank Pitcher Wm Zimmer Lawrence Warner Wm J Secor A.S. Ketcham Wm H Ketcham Morgan Secor There were Nine votes cast for Trustee. Morgan Secor received six votes and Lawrence Warner received three Morgan Secor was elected trustee by three Majority. Frank Pitcher was Elected Collector by one majority. There was 2.55 turned over to Morgan Secor. on what was left over on painting school hous[e]

There was a motion carried unanimously to raise $120 dollars for school purposes the ensuing year

The contract to furnish wood for the ensuing year was awarded to Morgan Secor. the wood to be fitted for the stove. for $9.00 dollars

There was a motion before the house which was carried that the trustee if he can make a bargain with [Cora?] Zimmer he hire her for teacher for the ensuing year.

Resolved that the meeting adjourn until the next anual meeting

W H Ketcham dist Clerk

[1900 October]

At a special meeting of the legal voters of school district No 5 in the town of Knox held at the school house in said district the following resolutions were passed

It was resolved that Wm J. Secor be chairman

The following named persons voted W H Ketcham David Vanderbelt Wm J Secor Morgan Secor Frank Pitcher ~~Frank~~ John Snyder L Warner Robert Oliver A.S. Ketcham Jas Armstrong

There was a motion before the house that we hire Adelia Secor to teach school in dist No 5 providing she gets a permit

There was three votes in ~~favor~~ opposition and three in favor There was a motion that the meeting adjourn

dated Oct 16th 1900

Wm H Ketcham dist Clerk

[1901 August]

At an anual meeting of the legal voters of school district No 5 of the town of Knox held at the school house in said district on the 6th day of August 1901 the following resolutions were passed

Resolved that Wm J. Secor be chairman

Resolved that Wm H Ketcham be clerk for the ensuing year

Frank Pitcher was elected trustee by six majority

It was resolved that Morgan Secor be collector for the ensuing year

The contract to furnish wood for the ensuing year fitted for the stove was awarded to Wm J Secor for Nine dollars & fifty cnets $9.50

It was resolved that that [sic] what money Morgan Secor has in his hands belonging to the district shall be applied for teachers wages

It was resolved that 125 dollars be raised by tax for school purposes the ensuing year

The meeting adjourned until the next anual meeting Wm H Ketcham dist clerk

[1902 August]

[This page is in pencil.]

At an anual meeting held at the school house in school district No 5 in the town of Knox on the 5th day of August 1902 The following resolutions were passed

Resolved that Wm J. Secor be chairman

Resolved that Wm H Ketcham be clerk for the ensuing year

Wm J. Secor was elected trustee for the ensuing year by a unanimous vote

Resolved that Clarence Quay be Collector for the ensuing year

It was voted on and carried that $100 dollars be raised by tax on property for school purposes the ensuing year

The contract to furnish the wood fitted for the stove was awrded to Wm J Secor for ten dollars $10-

Resolved that the meeting adjourn until the next anual meeting

Wm H. Ketcham} Dist Clerk

[1903 August]

Resolved that Franklin Pitcher acts as Chairman of School Meeting in Dis no. 5 in the town of Knox Albany Co on 11the day of August 1903 Four vote cast for William Ketcham Dis clerk. Three votes cast for William J Secor trustee for the ensueing year. three votes cast for William Zimer collector for the ensueing year

Four votes cast for raising $125.00 dol. for school purposes.

Contract let to W. J. Secor to furnish wood for the stove for the ensueing year for $12.00. Motion made that we adjurn to the next anual School Meeting,

Oct 10the 1903

[This page is in pencil.]

Motion made that William Zimer acts as chaireman [sic] of this meeting

Four votes casted [sic] that we hire Adelia Secor if we can get her _ Three yes one no,

Meetean [sic] will now be adjurned,

August the 2 1904

At the Anual School Meeting in Dis No.5. in the town of Knox Albany CO

Resolve that Danial [sic] S Quay act as chairman.

Five votes cast for Franklin Pitcher for clerk for the insueing year. [Six?] cotes [sic] cast four votes sast [sic] for William J. Secor and to cast for Sorense Warner for trustee [Six?] votes cast for Clarence Quay collector

Resolved that we allow William J Secor his [portion?] [on?] $12.50 libary. [Six?] votes cast. [Six?] votes cast for raising $125 more or less. [The word "Six" is consistently written "Sis."]

Contract let to W.J. Secor to furnish wood for the insueing year for $15.00.

resolve that we adjourn to the next anual meeting

September 7the 1904

[This page is in pencil.]

Special school Meeting

that W.J. Secor hire Alelia [sic] Secor for teacher. Nine votes cast for to hire her

Motion is made that we adjourn untill the Next anual School Meeting.

Knox August 1^{the} 1905
Anual School Meeting
In Dis No. 5
Resolved that Daniel S Quay act as Chairman of this Metting [sic]

Knox August 1 the 1905
Anua School Meeting
In Dis No 5
Resolved that Daniel S Quay act as Chairman of this Metting
Resolved that Franklin Pitcher act as Clerk for the Ensneing year Three for and One Against
Resolved that William J Secor act as Trustee for the Ensneing year vote Emmanous
Resolved that Daniel S Quay Act as Collecter for the Ensueing year vote Enmansous.
Resolved that we raise $125 dol for school purpsose.
Motion is made and seced that W J Secor furnish wood all redy for stove for $15.00.
Motion made and seconed that we adjourned untill the next annual school meeting

Resolved that Franklin Pitcher act as Clerk for the Ensueing year. Three for [Here the writer changed to pencil.] and one against

Resolved that William J Secor act as Trustee for the Ensueing year vote Enmanous [sic]

Resolved that Daniel S Quay Act as Colecter for the Ensueing year vote Enmansous [sic]

Reesolved [sic] that we raise $125 dol for school purpsose [sic]

Motion is made and seced that W J Secor furnish wood all redy for stove for $15.00. [It appears that a "2" was overwritten with the "5".]

Motion made and secened that we adjourned untill the next anual school meeting

[two blank pages]

[The following table was written near the back of the book; it appears to be the writing of Isaac Reamer who was clerk from 1875 to 1884.]

[This page is in pencil.]

Timber For the Shead, [Got. Out?]

6.	Posts	15.	feet	Long	9. by	10.	do.	[ ]	4 -
3.	Sills	20.	do.	do.	9. do.	10.	do.	--	3 -
1.	Sill	22.	do.	do.	9. do.	10.	do.	--	1 -
3.	Sleapers,	22.	do.	do.	flat			--	3 -
3.	Beams	20.	do.	do.	8. by	9.	do.		
4.	Loose Beams,	20.	do.		flat			--	4 -
3.	Gists,	22.	feet	do.	7. by	8.	do		-
1	Gist	22.	do.	do	10. do.	11.	do.		-

\- - - - - - - - - -

	feet	
4. Posts.	15.	-
3. Sills.	20.	-
1 Sill.	22.	
4 Beams,	20,	flat
3 Sleapers,	22.	Flat

Inside Back Cover:
Resolver
Resolved thus
[The following calculations are in pencil:]
850/12=7
144x700=1008 +11=10,19 Tax
[ ] S. Tax
40x7=280
700x40=2800
700x70=4,90,00 +5=4,95
4050x144=583200 +59=58,98 T
1019+495=15,14

Back Cover:
School District
No.5, Knox
Albany County,
1832

Index

[The Index does not include the contents of Appendix II.]

www.ingramcontent.com/pod-product-compliance
Ingram Content Group UK Ltd.
Pitfield, Milton Keynes, MK11 3LW, UK
UKHW041939190726
13854UKWH00004B/1678